teenage

degenerate

s.c. sterling

www.teenagedegenerate.com
www.facebook.com/teenagedegenerate

Please email questions or comments to sc@scsterling.com.

Thanks to my family and friends.

This book would not be possible without the following musicians and bands who gave me inspiration during the entire writing process.

A Day to Remember, AFI, Alice in Chains, Alkaline Trio, All Time Low, Authority Zero, the Beatles, Billy Talent, blink-182, Boys Like Girls, Brand New, Bruno Mars, Candlebox, Chuck Ragan, City and Colour, Coldplay, The Darlings, Dashboard Confessional, Eminem, Fallout Boy, Foo Fighters and Sonic Highways, Frank Sinatra, Frank Turner, The Fray, Fun., Green Day, Guns N' Roses, Ignite, Imagine Dragons, Jimmy Eat World, Joey Cape and Tony Sly, Johnny Cash, Kendrick Lamar, Macklemore and Ryan Lewis, Maroon 5, Metallica, Mumford and Sons, Muse, My Chemical Romance, Nathaniel Rateliff, New Found Glory, Nirvana, N.W.A, Oasis, Of Monsters and Men, One Republic, Pearl Jam, Pennywise, Pink Floyd, Queen, Radiohead, Rage Against the Machine, Rise Against, The Rolling Stones, Royal Blood, Slipknot, The Smashing Pumpkins, Stone Temple Pilots, Strung Out, Sublime, Sum 41, Third Eye Blind, Thirty Seconds to Mars, Tool, Twenty One Pilots, and Yellowcard.

Author's Note

Some names have been changed, some haven't. Some dates have been changed, some haven't. There are two sides to every story, this is mine.

de·gen·er·ate

adjective

1. having lost the physical, mental, or moral qualities considered normal and desirable; showing evidence of decline.

noun

1. an immoral or corrupt person.

verb

1. decline or deteriorate physically, mentally, or morally.

Summer 1996

Friday, July 5th

The first time I did crystal methamphetamine I was nineteen, sitting in the backseat of Jake's silver 1988 Oldsmobile Cutlass Ciera with my girlfriend, Leah, beside me. The rest of the crew was filled out with Jake in the driver's seat, Mark sitting shotgun, and Tony in the backseat with Leah and me.

We were parked in our favorite drinking and smoking location, which we had named Miller's Crossing. I was the oldest of the group, and Leah was the youngest at seventeen. We all still lived with our parents, so finding a place to drink, do drugs, and partake in debauchery was always a challenge. Miller's Crossing was the ideal destination.

On a map, the spot was off Oak Street and Montgomery Avenue in Littleton, Colorado, a suburb southwest of Denver. Oak dead-ended about a quarter mile to the north, and the only way to reach our parking spot was to turn off Montgomery from Miller, but that was over half a mile to the west. There was nothing but open fields to the south and east. At Oak's dead end, there was a single house, but no other homes were within a mile of us. I could have yelled at the top of my lungs, and not a soul outside our car would have heard me.

If a vehicle did turn down Montgomery, it meant one of two possibilities: the people who lived in the house on Oak were coming home, or the police were randomly patrolling the area. In the latter case, we would have to either ditch all the alcohol and illegal substances or elect someone to take the contraband and sprint for safety into the field.

That was Miller's best attribute: it allowed us half a mile to decide what to do. Luckily, in the two years we had been going there, we had never seen the headlights of an oncoming car.

Earlier in the evening, Mark had run into a guy that owed him eighty dollars for an acid deal they had done a few months previous. Mark fronted the guy twenty hits of LSD-25, and the guy promised he would pay Mark back a few days later. The guy had been avoiding Mark since that night, but the two finally ran into each other outside a gas station named Total. The guy did a pathetic job of explaining how he had been trying to get a hold of Mark.

"Dude, I paged you a bunch of times, but you never called me back, and I forgot your home number." He went into a sob story and asked Mark if he would be interested in negotiating a trade for the money he was owed.
"What kind of trade?" Mark asked.

The guy offered up a quarter of crystal meth and a quarter of cocaine in exchange for the money. Mark began calculating the exchange rates of coke and crystal versus the finest acid currently available. After a few moments, he put his hand out.

"You got yourself a deal," he said, as they shook hands.

Less than ten minutes after Mark walked out of the bathroom in Total with two baggies of white powder in his pocket, we were parked at Miller's Crossing. Jake barely had the car parked before Mark and Tony had snorted their respective lines. Jake and Leah followed suit. It was now my turn.

In my right hand I held the CD case for Rage Against the Machine's self-titled album. Grooves and scratch marks on its plastic surface told the stories of the numerous lines that had been cut out on it over time. My line was around four inches long and covered almost the entire length of the CD case. Underneath the cocaine, I could see the black and white album artwork of a Buddhist monk engulfed in flames.

In my left hand I held a tooter—the device used to snort meth, coke, heroin, or any other desired powder into your nose. Tooters can be anything from a rolled-up dollar bill to a hollowed-out pen or any other thinly shaped cylindrical item. In this case, it was a McDonald's plastic straw that had been cut into thirds.

To say that I was nervous would be an understatement. The CD case was shaking violently, shifting the cocaine from its perfectly straight line. I wasn't nervous about overdosing. (Don't get me wrong—having a heart attack and dying the first time I snorted anything would have been a shame.) Acutely aware of my extremely addictive personality, I was actually worried about liking it too much.

I had smoked marijuana almost every day since my junior year of high school, and I had been drinking a few nights a week for almost as long. Personally, I would have preferred to drink more often, but finding a willing buyer of booze for underage kids was more of an obstacle than purchasing weed. Marijuana was always only one or two phone calls away.

I looked up from the CD case, and everybody in the car had their eyes on me. Jake and Mark started a chant.

"Cannonball! Cannonball!"

It was a reference to the scene in *Caddyshack* where Carl, Bill Murray's character, hands a joint to Ty, played by Chevy Chase. Ty takes a hit off the joint, then Carl hands him a bottle of cheap wine to chase the marijuana.

Our version contained a revision. Instead of weed and alcohol, our cannonball required me to inhale a hit of crystal meth then snort a line of cocaine. This was a little more difficult than what Ty did, and it required concentration and timing. Naturally, lungs want to exhale before they inhale again.

"Cannonball! Cannonball!" Tony had joined the chant. He started punching the back of the headrest on the passenger seat.

I looked over to Leah, who was my last chance to escape this situation. Her smile confirmed that there was no turning back. Not only was I doing cocaine for the first time, but I was taking my first hit of crystal meth as well.

"See you guys in the emergency room," I said.

At that moment, I thought of Len Bias. Len was selected by the Boston Celtics as the second overall pick in the 1986 NBA Draft. Three days after he was drafted, he died of cardiac arrhythmia induced by a cocaine overdose. He was twenty-two. I remember watching the coverage of his death on the news with my mom and vowing never to do drugs.

Tony leaned toward me over Leah. He held a lighter and a newly prepared light bulb containing a few rocks of crystal meth. He was waiting for my signal.

I reluctantly nodded my head.

Tony flicked the lighter and held the flame a few inches below the bulb. It was the textbook position: if the flame was too far away, the meth would not get hot enough to melt into a gas. If the flame was too close, the meth could burn up and be wasted.

It took about ten seconds for the crystals to start vaporizing, and then the bulb slowly filled with a circular cloud of creamy white smoke. When it was about half-full, I knew it was the start of my countdown. Tony released the spark wheel on the lighter, and the flame disappeared.

I took a last glance at the others, hoping that someone would intervene. No such luck. I placed the tooter into the bulb, leaned forward, closed my eyes, and inhaled the smoke.

The chant resumed, but louder this time. "Cannonball! Cannonball!"

I did everything in my power not to cough out any smoke as I positioned the CD case under my nose, and only a few tiny clouds of smoke escaped my mouth. Inserting the tooter into my right nostril, I attempted to snort the massive line of cocaine, but I managed to finish only about half of it. My lungs felt like they were going to explode. I coughed out the remainder of the crystal smoke that my lungs had not absorbed.

Everyone erupted in a celebration that made the car shake from side to side. I handed the CD case to Leah and leaned back against the headrest. The speaker directly behind my head was playing the chorus of "Killing in the Name Of."

I don't want to sound cliché, but it was an amazing, euphoric feeling. I really can't explain how it felt. I guess if you've done it, you already know, and if you haven't, words really can't describe it. I understood how someone could lose their job, their family and their life over drugs.

Fuck, I was almost dead within ten months from it.

Saturday, July 6th

We spent the rest of the night at our favorite after-hours location, Denver International Airport. DIA was the newly constructed airport located northeast of Denver and about an hour from Miller's. It was the perfect location to explore while drunk, tripping on a hallucinogen, or in our case, high on powder.

For starters, the drive was a real time killer. Instead of being parked in a dirt lot, we were driving to a destination—something to get excited about. Additional benefits were that it was open 24-7/365, and an adult ID was not required for admission.

At two thirty in the morning, the lobby was virtually a ghost town except for the occasional janitor operating a floor buffer. We had complete run of the place, jumping from passenger train to passenger train, concourse to concourse.

A few years before this, Jake's older brother was working for an airline that gave him an all-access pass. He snuck Jake, myself, and a few other guys into the airport to give us a tour of DIA a few weeks before it opened to the public. We all dropped a few hits of acid on the drive there, and ended up driving a luggage cart down a newly paved runway at three in the morning.

This trip to DIA was not as eventful, and after a few hours we got bored and left. Jake dropped everyone off one by one until we were the last two remaining in the car. The conversation and laughter shifted into total silence.

At 5:05 a.m., I finally arrived home—well, my parents' home.

"Thanks, man. I'll talk to you later," I said to Jake, who started to drive off before I could shut the passenger door.

As I stumbled up the driveway, I glanced left to the sunrise breaking on the eastern horizon. It had been a long night and was going to be a longer day; I was scheduled to work in less than an hour. It wasn't the first time I pulled an all-nighter, but normally I was coming off an acid trip and still seeing visuals dancing around in my head. Luckily, Mark gave me a couple lines of crystal to do on my lunch break as a midday pick-me-up.

The moment I walked into my bedroom I decided to snort a line because there was no sense lying on my bed and waiting for the buzz of my alarm clock. Sleep was completely out of the question. I began searching for the proper tools to snort the meth while simultaneously dressing for work.

....

I worked as a courtesy clerk at a regional grocery store. My responsibilities were sacking groceries, collecting shopping carts, sweeping the floors, and any unpleasant tasks that no other employee wanted to do. A few months after I started, I had to clean a bathroom stall that had projectile shit all over the walls and floor.

Minimum wage was $4.25 an hour, but I made $4.63. After taxes, a forty-hour week netted me around $160. It doesn't seem like much, but I was still living at home with no rent, no car payment, no insurance, and no other bills of any substance.

I put a large portion of each paycheck into savings, and even at that minuscule wage I was able to accumulate a couple thousand dollars after a few years. Any cash that I didn't put into savings went to three things: alcohol, drugs, and music.

Although I was saving money, I had no idea why. I had no plans for college or any life after high school. I don't ever recall having a conversation with my parents about my future career ambitions. I considered attending college during my senior year of high school, so I took the ACT. I scored a 19 without studying for it, on zero sleep and dropping a hit of acid 14 hours before I picked up the pencil for the test.

I didn't blame my parents though; neither of them went to college. I think their highest aspirations for me were that I would work my way up the grocery store career ladder, get married, have a couple kids, retire as a deli manager after forty years, and call it a life.

....

My parents both grew up in towns that were gas station stops off Interstate 94 in western North Dakota. My dad was born and raised in a Podunk town that had a population of around 10,000 people. He was the fourth oldest of twelve children. My mom grew up in an even smaller Podunk town that peaked with a population of around 800. She was the youngest child of six.

They got married in the summer of 1971 and had my brother, Jim, the following summer. My dad worked as a meat cutter at the local grocery, and my mother watched Jim during the days and worked as a waitress at night.

A few months before I was born in the summer of 1976, they packed up a trailer and headed west to Portland, Oregon.

I was raised in a small two-bedroom apartment where my brother and I shared a bedroom and slept in a wooden bunk bed my parents purchased from a secondhand thrift store. Jim had the top bunk, and I envisioned it collapsing onto me every night when I closed my eyes. My dad continued working as a meat cutter, and my parents doubled as leasing agents at our run-down apartment complex to receive a discount on our monthly rent. My weekly highlight was our Friday night family dinners at McDonald's or Kentucky Fried Chicken.

In the winter of 1988, my dad received a job offer at a brand-new grocery store in Denver, Colorado. After a lengthy family discussion, my parents concluded the family would be moving east.

Within a few weeks, we had our moving day confirmed. I said my goodbyes to my elementary school friends, we packed up every possession into a twenty-foot U-Haul truck, and we cut our ties with the West Coast. We drove the 1,200 miles in two days and arrived in Denver in January of 1988.

My parents purchased a small three-bedroom, two-bathroom house in the town of Morrison, another suburb of southwest Denver. For the first time I had my own room, as well as a garage and fenced yard with a patio.

The mortgage required my parents to have additional income, and that required my mother to get a full-time job as a housekeeper for a major hotel chain. We lived paycheck to paycheck and had very little extra money for added amenities or family vacations. My parents did their best to give my brother and me a lower-middle-class upbringing.

Jim graduated high school two years after we moved to Colorado and enlisted in the Army the following year. He got shipped off to Fort Campbell in Kentucky in December of 1990, a few months after the start of the Gulf War.

With my brother on the other side of the country and both my parents working forty to fifty hours a week, I basically became a latchkey kid. I had no curfew or real parental supervision, coming and going as I pleased as long as I left a note.

The first time I got drunk I was fourteen, and I smoked marijuana a few months later.

. . . .

I arrived to work a few minutes before 6:00 a.m. I clocked in, fastened my red apron, pinned on my name tag, and walked to the closest register to bag up various items for the early-morning shoppers.

10

Saturdays were normally the busiest days, and that combined with snorting a line every two hours, made work fly by. Before I knew it, my shift was over.

After I clocked out, I walked to the pharmacy. I was tired, but I knew there was no possibility of sleep without pharmaceutical assistance. I located the sleeping-pill section and slipped a box of Unisom into the pocket of my apron. My philosophy was if it could fit into the pockets of my apron, it was free. I walked back, past the line of registers, to the main entrance and the freedom of the outside world.

Luckily, my parents lived less than ten minutes from the store because I was starting to crash from being awake for over thirty-five hours. When I got home, I walked straight into my basement bedroom, sat down on the edge of my bed, opened up the box of Unisom, and removed four pills. I then picked up a half-empty bottle of Jim Beam that I had stashed next to my nightstand. I popped the pills into my mouth and chased them with a few shots of whiskey, deciding to swallow one additional pill to ensure I was going to be completely comatose.

I placed disc one of Pink Floyd's *The Wall* into my five-disc CD changer, fluffed my pillows, and rested my head on top of them. My breathing subdued, and I began to drift in and out of consciousness.

Sunday, July 14th

I won last minute Warped Tour tickets from a radio station giveaway in a Walgreens parking lot. Warped Tour is an annual alternative/punk rock festival that crisscrosses the United States and Canada. The lineup featured Deftones, Pennywise, NOFX, and twenty other bands I had never heard of or had any desire to see.

The concert was at the world-famous outdoor venue Red Rocks Amphitheater. Red Rocks was practically in my back yard, and if it weren't for the Dinosaur Ridge mountain formation, I could see it from my parent's backyard.

Red Rocks has hosted almost every major rock band over the last forty years, including the Beatles, Jimi Hendrix, The Grateful Dead, and Dave Mathews Band. U2 recorded *Under a Blood Red Sky* there on a rain-soaked evening in 1983.

My high school graduation took place at Red Rocks in June of 1995. Jake and I woke up a few hours before the scheduled starting time, got dressed in our cap and gown then smoked weed nonstop until we arrived. I distinctly remember two things from the three-hour long ceremony:

1. After two years of middle school and four years of high school, I had never met the two people I was sitting between and with whom I shared the closest proximity of last names.
2. I convinced myself that I was too high to walk down the stairs and became paranoid about tripping while I walked across the stage to get my diploma from the principal.

Those two items basically sum up my entire high school career.

Before we went to Red Rocks, we needed to stock up on supplies. Mark had a half gram of crystal hidden in his bedroom. Obtaining it required some planning because his mother was home, and if he returned, she would not allow him to leave again unless he had a valid reason—going to a concert was not acceptable for her. She was overprotective and thought everyone Mark associated with was a bad influence on him. If she had a feeling he was hanging out with me, he would not be allowed to leave the house. We started brainstorming ideas to deceive his mother.

"Fuck, I got it! I'll just tell her I'm going to a GED study group, and I need to grab my study guide. That'll work right?" Mark asked.

I shrugged my shoulders, unsure of the possible outcome.

I parked a few blocks from Mark's house and watched as he turned the corner. I had serious doubts that his mother would be dumb enough to fall for a study group on a Sunday afternoon in the summer. On the other hand, Mark was an exceptional liar. I had once seen him sell individual Smarties for five-dollars after he convinced a group of kids that each piece of candy contained a drop of acid.

After about ten minutes of switching between radio stations, Mark appeared, skipping along the sidewalk. His lying skills outweighed her common sense.

"She fucking bought it! Well, at least for the moment. Let's get the fuck out of here!" he yelled as he jumped into my truck.

I envisioned her making a phone call to the library to follow up on his story and realizing that there was no such study group and that she got duped. He would have to deal with the consequences later, but that wasn't my concern. I started my truck and sped out of the neighborhood.

We made a quick stop at Safeway to purchase tin foil and a package of lighters, along with hotdog buns and yellow mustard to mask the drug-related purchases. We were in and out of Safeway in a few minutes then made the short drive to my house.

My parents were in Fort Collins, almost an hour and a half north of Denver, visiting my aunt and uncle. I knew the house would be empty, allowing me the freedom to properly prepare my concert survival backpack.

Mark began cutting up lines on the kitchen table while I ran downstairs to my bedroom to gather supplies. I stuffed my backpack with nine cans of Miller Genuine Draft, the remaining bottle of Jim Beam, a pint of McCormick Vodka, and three cans of Sprite. This arsenal, along with the meth Mark had, would suffice for a couple hours of concert tailgating. I always thought it was better to be over prepared in case of an emergency.

"Do you think this is enough?" I asked as I opened the backpack.
"Yeah, I think we're good."

Within minutes of leaving, we were traveling on Colorado Highway 470 and only a few miles south of the town of Morrison. Morrison is at the base of Red Rocks and a tourist destination that includes restaurants, bars, and random gift shops. The town has only two stoplights that become a traffic nightmare after shows. By the time we drove through Morrison, the streets were almost empty.

We were some of the last people to arrive, and the attendant directed us to the lower south lot, the farthest parking location— almost a half-mile walk uphill to reach the main entrance.

The parking lot was a ghost town except for the occasional concert-goer who was too inebriated to make the hike to the entrance. That was fine by me. It gave us the freedom to smoke meth without hiding behind the dashboard.

Mark dumped a few large crystal rocks into the makeshift tin foil pipe, and flicked it to arrange the rocks in the desired position. He started smoking without hesitation. I opened a MGD and watched him inhale three consecutive hits before he handed the pipe and tooter to me.

We kept passing the meth back and forth for almost ten minutes and then started incorporating shots of Jim Beam between handoffs of the pipe.

I faintly heard music echoing off the surrounding rock formations. That was our cue. I took one final hit, exited my truck, and performed a few quick calf stretches in preparation for the climb to reach the main gate.

"Rock and roll!" I shouted as I slammed the truck door shut.

Wednesday, July 17th

July 16th was Jim's birthday, and I had completely forgotten about it. I think he turned twenty-four. I had been planning to get him a present, but I had no idea what to get. Even though he was my brother, I barely knew him. He was almost six years older than me, and we were never that close. He graduated from high school while I was still in middle school.

He did teach me a few things: how to pass rush an offensive lineman, how to drive, and how to properly smoke weed out of a bong—everything a little brother should know.

I also owed him for the complete and total freedom that I received from my parents.

While Jim was still living at home, he drank a lot and came home drunk most nights. That usually resulted in a verbal and physical altercation between him and my father directly outside my bedroom door.

One evening, I attempted to be the mediator and break up a fight. In the process, I was accidently hit with an elbow square in the face and dropped to the carpet with blood gushing from my nose.

After that, my dad never checked on Jim again and never checked on me. I think he felt guilty for hitting one of his kids and did not want to be put into that situation again.

Sunday, July 21st

I was walking up an aisle at work when I recognized Caleb, a guy I went to high school with. I hid behind a product display and was about to turn around when he greeted me with a middle-finger wave. I had a few classes with him, and we played football together, but I never liked him. He was the stereotypical jock type that I hated. I greeted him with a fake smile and began the obligatory small talk.

"I'm watching my aunt's apartment for a few days. Do you want to get a few people together to come over?"

I still didn't like the guy, but I never passed on a place to party.

"I'll hit you up when I am off, and we will work out the details," I said as I continued up the aisle.

I got off a few hours later and strolled to the payphone outside, quarters in hand. I paged Jake and Mark then leaned back against the brick wall, awaiting a return call. I was in no rush. My bootlegger was a cashier named Frank, and he didn't get off for another half hour.

I preferred to use Frank because he never said no, never asked me to purchase him anything, and always returned with exact change. He was also fucking crazy, and when I say crazy, I mean insane.

One night Frank hosted a small party in his apartment that he shared with his twin brother, Doug. About ten people were there, drinking and playing card games. I brought a girl I was hoping to fuck later that evening.

Without warning, Frank gathered everyone into the living room around the TV and pressed play on the VCR. After a few unfocused, blurry moments, the homemade video came into focus and revealed Frank and Doug mutilating a dead cat on a deserted road in the mountains. I wasn't sure if the cat was real at first, but a close-up of the cat confirmed it was no prop.

They were picking it up with a shovel, throwing it across the road and used an ax to hack off parts of its tail. The grand finale was them loading a handgun and shooting the feline a few times in the head and torso.

I looked back at Frank in complete horror, and he was just standing in the kitchen with an eerie smile on his face. The party concluded a few minutes after the tape ended.

Needless to say, I didn't get the opportunity to fuck that girl. In fact, she never spoke to me again after that night.

Since then, I kept my distance from Frank—except for alcoholic purchases. I guess being an underage alcoholic made me resort to drastic measures like associating with potential serial killers.

The phone finally rang, and I quickly answered it. It was Jake, and we put together a plan for the night's activities.

"Go home and get ready. I'll be there in a half," Jake stated.

After Frank had purchased my alcohol, I drove home, showered, got dressed, and was sitting on the sidewalk in front of my house in under twenty-five minutes. I tossed pebbles into the street waiting for Jake to arrive.

I finally heard his car from around the corner; the engine made an awful squealing sound each time Jake pressed on the gas. I stood up and checked the time on my pager; he was only a few minutes late.

"Sorry, I was waiting for Samantha to call me," he said through the open passenger window.
"Samantha?"
"I think you know her," he responded.

I did, in fact, know who she was. I just didn't know they were talking. I had seen her in the neighborhood and at the park a few times. She was a couple years younger and going to be a freshman when school started back up in the fall. She was gorgeous, and I was somewhat jealous Jake was hooking up with her even though I had a girlfriend.

"Yeah, I think so."
"Cool. She wants to hang out."

We picked up Samantha, then Mark and another friend, Andre, and arrived at the apartment complex a little after ten. After pounding on the wrong door and scaring an elderly, senile woman, we found the correct building and apartment.

The party consisted of Caleb, Jake, Samantha, Mark, Andre, myself, two cases of Old Style, a bottle of Southern Comfort, and a quarter bag of weed. I also had a minuscule amount of meth that Mark forgot in my ashtray after Warped Tour. I didn't have enough for everyone, so I was keeping it a secret. My plan was to snort lines throughout the night then give the rest to whoever was going to drive home as an aid to sober up.

The first few hours were like any other party I'd been to since freshman year: drinking, doing shots, listening to music, and playing drinking games. A newly rolled joint was passed around the circle every half hour or so.

As the night progressed, we divided into groups: Jake and Samantha retreated into the bedroom, Caleb and Mark played poker in the kitchen, and Andre and I argued about music.

Andre was the type of person that would take a stance on a topic and fight tooth and nail that he was right. If he was standing in front of a red house, he could declare it was blue and make arguments to support his side. It could be entertaining at times, but at other times I wanted to strangle him

Tonight's topic was 1970s music, and that it was the pinnacle of rock music, and that it would never be surpassed.

"Pink Floyd *Dark Side of the Moon* and *The Wall*. Led Zeppelin *IV* and *Physical Graffiti*. The Stones, the Clash, and Sex Pistols. Fuck, I could go on forever," he said as he took a hit off a joint.
"The Sex Pistols and the Clash? Two of the most overrated bands in history," I said, laughing.

He was about to erupt with a rebuttal when …

BAM, BAM, BAM!

Everyone looked at each other and back to the front door.

I ran over to the stereo and pressed pause, and the room was instantly silent. I thought the noise could have been coming from the headboard in the bedroom.

BAM, BAM, BAM!

"Lakewood Police Department, open the door!" a voice yelled.

I began thinking of an exit strategy: bum rush the cops, jump out the tiny bathroom window, hide in the hallway closet.

"Everyone be cool," Caleb whispered as he tip-toed to the front door.

That's when I remembered Caleb was a 911 dispatcher for Lakewood Police Department. A few hours ago he told us a story about how he was friends with most of the Lakewood police officers. He even bragged that he got pulled over drunk a few weeks earlier and should have received a DUI but talked his way out of it because he was a dispatcher.

"One second," Caleb yelled.
"Should we hide the alcohol?" I whispered.

"No, don't worry about it. We will be fine," he said, his voice full of confidence.

I got off the couch and made my way to the kitchen, so that I wouldn't be in plain sight once the front door opened.

Caleb opened the door only a few inches, making his face visible to the cops outside. He started explaining that he worked for the same police department as them.

"I don't know who you are, so open this door, go sit down, and shut the fuck up," one officer yelled.

That was a serious problem. I had enough meth in my pocket to put me in jail for a substantial amount of time, and if I knew Jake, he was most likely fucking a minor in the bedroom and committing statutory rape.

I had to decide if I was going to alert Jake about the police presence or escape into the bathroom to flush the meth down the toilet. I decided on the selfish route. I'd save myself then save Jake if time permitted.

I ran down the hallway and kicked the bathroom door open Chuck Norris style while I simultaneously searched my pockets for the tiny Ziploc baggie. I searched both pockets multiple times, and finally discovered the baggie in my right pocket. I thought about hiding it in the bathroom but decided against it. I kissed the baggie and flushed the toilet as it hit the water.

I ran out of the bathroom to the bedroom door.

"Are you guys drinking or smoking marijuana tonight?" I overheard a cop ask from the living room.

I pushed the door open and saw Jake's bare ass bouncing up and down on the bed with Samantha completely naked on all fours.

They both swung their heads around in unison, and he was about to yell at me when I put my hand up to stop him.

"The 5-0 is here so you guys might want to stop fucking and put some clothes on."

I quietly shut the door, attempting not to alert the cops of the activity going on in the bedroom. Then I walked back into the living room where I was promptly instructed by one of the police officers to sit down. He then turned his attention back to Caleb.

"I'm not going to ask you again. Is there anyone else in this apartment?" asked the cop, sticking an index finger in Caleb's face. Fearful of losing his job, Caleb answered as honestly as he could. "I believe there are two people having sexual intercourse in the bedroom, sir."

I wanted to punch Caleb in the face. That dumb mother-fucker essentially put Jake's penis right back inside Samantha.

"Go sit the fuck down!" the cop instructed Caleb as he swiftly walked to the bedroom door.

I crossed my fingers, praying that my warning was enough time for them to get dressed and proper.

"Lakewood Police Department! I am giving you five seconds to open the door or else I am coming in."

I could see him start the countdown in his head. 5….4…..3…..2….

Jake swung open the door and stood there fully clothed, hair styled, with a smile. He looked composed and not like he was just having sex less than sixty seconds before the cop knocked on the door. Possible disaster averted.

"What were the two of you doing in here?"
"Talking." Jake responded.

"Only talking? Nothing else? You guys were not having sexual relations in there?"

"No sir, I am a virgin," Jake said with a straight face.

I had to bite my lip not to burst out in laughter. The cop examined Jake up and down before telling him and Samantha to join me on the couch.

The next hour consisted of the cops documenting our personal information and handing out minor-in-possession tickets one by one. After they had finished writing the tickets, they told Andre and Caleb to pour the remaining alcohol down the kitchen sink.

Since Samantha was a minor, she was out after curfew and the cops had to escort her home. I imagined her parents would not be happy to have a 2:00 a.m. visit from the police telling them that their daughter was out getting drunk. I didn't envy her. They gave us a final warning before they left.

"And don't even think about leaving this apartment because if one of you steps as much as a foot into the hallway, I'm going to arrest all of you!" the officer yelled as he slammed the front door.

We sat in silence for the next twenty minutes or so until Caleb spoke.

"You guys have to go."

I was about ready to suggest that, but I was worried that the cops were waiting for us. I was willing to take that risk.

We just needed to figure out one important item: who was going to drive. We quickly came to the consensus that we were at the same level of inebriation, and the decision would be determined by an old-fashioned game of rock, paper, scissors.

I beat Jake with rock and Andre with scissors in the first two games, so I was safe. Jake and Andre glared at each other then slapped their fists into their palms to begin the countdown. Jake played scissor while Andre played paper, and just like that, the fate of our safety was determined by a playground game.

"Fuck!" Andre shouted as he threw his hands up in the air.

I was secretly relieved because I considered Andre the most talented drunk driver of our group. He made complete stops, used turn signals, didn't swerve, and always drove 5 mph under the speed limit. If we got pulled over while Andre was driving, odds were it was not because of his driving.

We exited the apartment and made a mad-dash to the entry door that opened to the parking lot. We investigated the lot as well as the adjoining street for any sign of police activity. The coast looked clear, so we ran the last fifty feet to Jake's Oldsmobile.

Andre did a quick inspection of the vehicle to ensure the headlights, tail lights, and blinkers were in proper working condition. He found no problems and gave us a thumbs-up to announce his approval.

In less than a minute, we were driving out of the parking lot. A quick right onto Jewel Avenue followed by a left onto Kipling Parkway, and it was less than a ten-minute drive until we reached the safe confines of the Lakehurst Park and Trappers Glenn subdivisions, our home turf.

"Don't say a fucking word! I need to concentrate!" Andre shouted, his hands secured at the ten and two positions on the steering wheel.

I felt obliged to grant his request, so I fastened my seat belt, closed my eyes, and leaned back as Andre turned up the stereo. The opening drumbeat and bass line of "Creep" by Radiohead echoed through the car speakers.

Saturday, July 27th

I woke up a little before noon and remained in bed for twenty minutes contemplating leaving my house. I was still upset about getting the MIP ticket and was convinced I would receive a hefty fine with numerous hours of community service. I guess it could have been worse; the cops could have caught me with that bag of meth.

I finally sat up on the edge of my bed, grabbed the TV remote, and started flipping through channels. Noon on a Saturday in July doesn't offer the highest quality of TV options. I was changing the channel every few seconds until something finally caught my eye.

Well, here in Atlanta, joy and celebration quickly turned to fear and death after an explosion in the Olympic Centennial Park early this morning. Authorities say it was a crude pipe bomb that exploded near the main entertainment stage.

I was in disbelief. I had just watched Muhammad Ali light the Olympic torch at the Summer Olympics opening ceremony the previous week. As I continued watching, facts emerged about the bombing.

The park was packed with thousands of spectators, athletes, news personnel, and workers who were there to watch a free concert after a full day of Olympic events. A custom-built pipe bomb filled with three-inch nails and screws exploded in the town square minutes before the concert. The explosion killed one person; another died of a heart attack while he was running to film the scene, and over 100 were hurt with various degrees of injuries.

I was glued to CNN for the next few hours, watching eye-witness reports and interviews with police officers, doctors, and government officials. President Bill Clinton spoke, calling the bombing "an evil act of terror."

I finally got to a breaking point and could no longer watch the news. I was sick to my stomach. I just wanted to get a release and forget about everything I had just witnessed.

I called Mark, and we developed a plan to get crystal and get high. I picked him up a little after 8:00 p.m., and we started our exploration around Littleton seeking out crystal. First, we stopped at Mark's normal dealer; he was out. We then drove to his backup dealer; she wasn't home. We then drove to a Conoco gas station so Mark could make a few pages.

After ten minutes with no phone activity, I started to think a crystal purchase was not going to be possible. It was 9:20, and I promised Leah I would pick her up from a friend's house before 10:00.

Finally, the phone rang. Mark lunged at the receiver, almost tripping over the curb.

"It's Mark."

Mark intently listened.

"A half."

Another pause.

"Perfect. See you in a few minutes!"

Mark hung up the phone and ran back to my truck.

"Bear Creek Apartments. Let's go!" Mark said.

The Bear Creek Apartments were almost exactly halfway between our location and where Leah was. If everything went smoothly, I would have crystal in my possession and be able to pick her up before 10:00. The problem was that nothing ever went smoothly when Mark was involved.

The drive to the apartment complex took less than ten minutes. I parked in a back spot away from the sidewalk and buildings.

"Hurry! I am only waiting ten minutes!" I said.
"I'll be back in five."

We both knew that was a lie. Mark got out of my truck and disappeared into the darkness of the courtyard that was scattered with trash cans, random shopping carts and a swing set that was missing the swings. It was 9:35.

Time stops when you're waiting for drugs, especially in a dark, isolated, somewhat dangerous parking lot. Searching for activities to occupy my time, I started looking away from the apartments. From my vantage point, I could see Bear Creek High School, the school I graduated from.

There I was, sitting alone in my truck, hoping to score a bag of crystal, while a majority of the classmates I graduated with were probably back home from their freshman year of college, preparing for their sophomore year. I felt despicable.

I decided to walk to the Mini-Mart that was across the street because I wanted to call Leah to let her know that I was running late. When I arrived at the pay phone, I realized that I didn't have any quarters to make the call.

"Shit!" I said as I hung up the receiver and walked into the Mini-Mart.

A doorbell rang as I entered the store, and a Middle-Eastern man stood up from behind the counter.

"Hey man, can I get some change?" I politely asked.
"You have to buy something."
"Are you serious?"
"Yes, sir," he said, nodding fiercely.

I paused for a moment, and attempted to regain my composure.

"Please, I just need to make a phone call, man."
"Sir, you have to buy something."

I was done being nice.

"You dumb, motherfucking camel jockey!"
"Get out of my store before I call the authorities!"
"Fuck you, cocksucker!" I yelled as I ran out of the store.

As I ran across the street, I began to worry that he actually did call the cops, so I took an alternative route back to my truck as a precaution.

When I returned, I sat down and leaned against my front tire until my breathing felt normal. I calculated that my adventure took at least twenty minutes, and Mark should be returning any minute. I stood up, entered my truck, turned on the ignition and patiently waited for the time to appear on my stereo.

9:43. Eight fucking minutes! Time had officially stopped. The life of a drug addict can be separated into two components: doing drugs and waiting to do drugs.

I decided to sit in my truck and wait. I had no choice but to wait. Leah would have to wait as well. Everyone and everything would have to be put on pause until our drug transaction was complete.

At 10:21, I finally recognized a shadow that resembled Mark. I decided if that wasn't him, I was leaving. An hour was my limit for tonight. Luckily for both of us, it was him.

....

About twenty minutes later Leah, her friend Lacy, Mark, and myself were all crammed into the bench seat of my truck with no destination. I needed a plan. I didn't want to be driving throughout

28

Lakewood with a pocket full of meth, two underage girls, and four people in the cab of a truck without the required number of seat belts.

I continued driving west on Alameda in the direction of Dinosaur Ridge with no luck. Searching for a suitable spot to smoke meth uninterrupted is harder than it seems. I was about to give up when a parking lot appeared out of nowhere. I slowed down to read the sign: "Hayden Park and Green Mountain."

"Holy fuck, how lucky could we get? This spot is perfect!" I shouted.

The parking lot was used as a starting point for mountain bikers and hikers before their journey up Green Mountain or Dinosaur Ridge. The lot was probably full during the day, but there was no reason to park here after sunset.

I turned off my lights and drove in the lot. My theory for turning off my lights was not a well-thought-out plan; I figured if my lights were off, no one could see us. The problem with that was I could not see anyone either.

I navigated into the southeast corner of the lot and reversed my truck up against a split-rail fence. It was pitch-black and felt like we were the only living souls for miles. It took a few moments for our eyes to adjust to the darkness.

Out my window and to my left was a grass field with weeds a few feet tall, some aspen trees, and a few random large boulders. A wolf howled in the distance. This location seemed like a hidden gem. I was already planning on it being our debauchery location for the foreseeable future.

While I was admiring my discovery, Mark was cutting out four lines. The girls were mesmerized with the powder and his razor work, like an artist painting his masterpiece. He was chopping and maneuvering back and forth until he had four lines that were the exact same width, length, and height.

Mark was about to snort his line when the darkness was interrupted by lustrous red and blue lights of a police car that was rapidly approaching my truck. In all my excitement of finding the perfect location, I must have overlooked him sitting in the darkness patiently waiting. I knew I should have circled the lot once to confirm it was empty and safe. I was about to pay the consequences for being sloppy.

I pictured him sitting in his car and watching us drive in and park, licking his lips in anticipation of confronting adolescents committing minor misdemeanors.

"Fucking asshole," I muttered.

Mark quickly moved his right hand to the door handle, and I instantly grabbed his free hand. I knew he was thinking about making a run for it.

"Don't fucking do it," I whispered under my breath.

If he ran, I would pay the penalty, and I could only picture two possible scenarios playing out:

1. Mark runs and gets away. The cop would be irate that Mark escaped him, and he would take out all his frustration on me. I would have zero chance of talking my way out of the situation. The night would include guaranteed jail time and probably a few punches to the abdomen after I was handcuffed.
2. Mark runs and gets tackled a half mile up the trail. From my experience with cops, they like as little physical activity as possible. The higher their heart rate increases, the more criminal charges that accumulate. The cop would definitely call in backup, possibly a drug-sniffing dog, and they would discover the meth.

Both scenarios ended with me in jail, and I wanted to avoid that at all costs. I knew if we played it perfectly, we might have a slim chance of driving out of here with a warning and a slap on the wrist. That was a big fucking might!

"Let me do the talking," I whispered.

Leah and Lacy nervously nodded.

"What the fuck do you want me to do with this?" Mark spit out the side of this mouth.

In all my preparation, I forgot the meth on top of the CD case resting on Mark's lap. That was going to pose a problem.

I looked at the police car without turning my head, attempting to make visual contact with the cop, but the headlights and sirens blinded me. I had no idea if he was watching us, looking at his computer, or doing a crossword puzzle. I had a feeling he was just waiting for us to make a mistake.

I slowly reached over Leah and Lacy and picked the CD case up off Mark's lap. My hand was steady like I was detonating a bomb. My fear was that I would dump the crystal on Leah's or Lacy's lap. After about twenty stress-filled seconds, I had the CD resting on my thigh.

The easiest part was complete; now it was on to the difficult part. My crudely developed plan was to fling the CD case out the window when the cop got out of his car. I figured I would have a few moments when he would look away, giving me a small window to safely toss the case into the grassy field. I had one chance to get this right, and my timing had to be impeccable.

If he did not see me throw the CD case, he would never find it because he only had access to the passenger side of my truck. To reach the driver's side, he would have to climb a fence and venture into the grass and weeds. I had a feeling he would only do that if he had reason to.

Since I couldn't see anything in his direction, I would have to listen for the car door to open. This required complete silence in the cab of the truck.

"Everyone shut the fuck up," I mumbled without moving my lips.

I lowered my head and moved it to the right, attempting to get a better listening angle. The cab was so quiet I couldn't even hear anyone else breathing.

I looked down and noticed the CD case was Nirvana's *In Utero*. I loved this album, and I really didn't want to lose it. I started thinking of ways that I could get rid of the meth and keep the album. After a few ill-advised thoughts, I decided against it. Jail time outweighed any CD. If I made it out of here, I would go buy it again. If I didn't, it would most likely be used as evidence, so I would get it back when I was released from jail.

I started to raise the case to the base of the window seal. My hand started to shake. I was fucking scared.

I finally heard the car door open and commenced my plan.

Mark made an impromptu move and shifted forward, providing a little cover. I raised my arm, flicked my wrist, and flung the case as far as I could out the window. I watched it peacefully glide through the dark sky, and it briefly settled my nerves. I took a deep breath then leaned toward the glove box to retrieve my proof of insurance and registration.

I was waiting for him to run toward the truck with his gun pointed. I waited but, it never happened.

"What are you guys doing here after hours?" he said, shining a flashlight directly into our eyes.

32

I was speechless. My plan never progressed to him asking that question. I was going to have to pull something out of thin air.

"We're just taking in the beautiful view officer. The stars look so much better out here than they do in the city."

He stepped closer and shined the spotlight in everyone's face, one by one, starting with Mark. He was trying to break one of us.

"You guys wouldn't be drinking or smoking any weed out here would you?"
"No!" we all said in unison shaking our heads back and forth.

I couldn't believe he asked the wrong fucking question. I was positive if he would have mentioned anything about meth, one of us would have cracked, or he would have seen right through us.

No, officer, we were not here to get drunk or smoke a bowl. Our sole purpose for being here is to do crystal methamphetamine. He pitched a fastball right over home plate, and we hit a 500-foot home run.

I knew he never saw the Nirvana CD case flying over the western wheatgrass under the stars. He followed up with a few more rudimentary questions, but I knew we were scot-free. I was no longer picturing myself spending the night in the Jefferson County Jail, which was a great feeling.

He handed back my license, insurance, and registration and started walking back to his car when he suddenly stopped to give us one last piece of advice.

"Next time, you guys should bring a couple flashlights and hike up Dinosaur Ridge after sunset. The views from up there are amazing, but remember the park closes at 10:00 p.m., so please leave before that."
"Thank you, officer, I'll remember that next time. Have a great night," I said with a smile.

33

I turned on the ignition, pulled the gear shifter into drive, and slowly drove to the entrance of the lot. As I flipped on my turn signal, I became so ecstatic that I broke into song.

"I'm not like them, but I'll try to pretend! The fucking sun is gone, but I have a light! The CD case is in the field and I'm still having fun! I think I'm dumb or maybe just fucking happy!"

Tuesday, July 30th

Mark, Tony, Jake, Andre, Craig, and I had tickets to see Pantera and White Zombie at Red Rocks. This was the first summer concert that all six of us attended together, so we were excited, and when I say excited, I mean our objective was to get so fucked up we would barely remember being at the concert.

We arrived in the parking lot around 2:00 p.m. with a cooler full of booze and a backpack full of drugs. We spent the next few hours sitting in the bed of my truck, drinking, snorting meth and attempting to attract females to partake in our pre-show party. There were no takers except for a fat girl that Mark propositioned to flash her tits in exchange for a Coors Light. After he saw her topless, he had a change of heart.

"Bitch, those titties are definitely not worth a beer! Let me see if I have any change in my pocket," he yelled at her.
"Fuck you, asshole!" she yelled back.

We all laughed at her expense as she walked away.

An hour before showtime we decided to trek up the stairs to the entrance. Forty minutes and three smoke breaks later we were twenty feet from the main gate.

I started doing my customary pre-security check for anything illegal. When you get as fucked up as we do before shows, you never know what could be hiding in a pocket. Even a roach would, at the least, get my concert ticket confiscated. I reached into my pocket and felt the top seal of a baggie. I dropped my head in disappointment.

"Fuck, I forgot to leave the meth in my truck."
"Just sneak it in," Mark said.
"I am not going to risk getting caught with that shit," I quickly responded.

There was no way I was going to attempt to sneak past a security pat-down with meth in my possession. I knew the odds were slightly in my favor because security guards always did a piss-poor job searching for contraband. It wasn't worth risking it though. With my luck I would get the security guard who failed the police academy and treated this job like he was a real cop. There seemed to be one of those guys at every show.

"Anybody want to run back to the truck?" I sympathetically asked.
"Fuck you!" Mark said.
"Nada." Tony responded.
"I guess I will," Craig volunteered.

We started our journey back to the parking lot a few hundred feet below and about a half mile to the south. This was not going to be an easy walk down. The platform was only about ten feet wide, and thousands of people were marching their way up, shoulder to shoulder, in the opposite direction.

We were the assholes going against traffic, weaving side-to-side to avoid coked out metal heads, wasted stoners, and inebriated girls in high heels for the sake of fashion. The herd got denser as we reached the halfway point; there seemed to be no end in sight. I stopped to catch my breath and seriously contemplated throwing the meth over the railing.

"Do you just want to ditch it and turn around?" I asked Craig.
"Fuck that!" Craig said, firmly grasping my shoulder. "I'll snort that shit off the fucking railing before I'll let you throw it away! Let's keep going. We're almost out of the weeds."

I really admired his determination because it would have ruined my night if I would have actually tossed it below.

Craig lowered his head and shoulders and started to plow his way through the crowd, not worrying about who was in his way—male or female, adult or child. He didn't give a fuck; he was on a mission. He created an opening, and I followed his lead.

36

"Fucking assholes," some guy yelled as he punched me in the middle of my back.

Neither of us turned around or cared.

....

Craig moved to Colorado in the summer of 1994 from Southern California. He lived with his mom, stepdad, and two siblings directly across the street from Jake's parents.

Shortly after Craig moved to Denver, he became friends with a guy named Justin. I only met Justin a couple times, but he always intimidated me. He was the type of guy that could snap at any moment for any reason. I kept my mouth shut when I was around him. I didn't want to be anywhere near him when he did snap.

In October of 1995, Craig and Justin were on a five-day meth binge.

Here is a breakdown of the first five days of continuous meth usage.

Days 1 and 2: This is why people become addicted to meth. Your senses feel heightened, both mentally and physically. You feel invincible, like you can accomplish anything. This is also the ambitious tweaker stage—you're going to write a novel, invent the next great gadget, or build an addition onto your house.

Day 3: The body is trying to adjust to seventy-two hours of no sleep and, little or no food. It's starting to take a toll on movement and reaction times. Everything seems to be in slow motion. The brain is too high to sleep but too tired to function. Continued intake of meth still results in a high, but with each line the "high time" begins to dwindle, and that shortens the meth intake intervals.

Day 4: You become irritable, anxious, paranoid, and really start hallucinating—and not the enjoyable hallucinations produced from acid or mushrooms. These hallucinations are something out of a horror movie. You hear noises; start seeing movements in shadows, people staring and talking about you, cops following you; and your best friend starts plotting against you. I would suggest that if you plan on staying up for four days, have as little contact with the outside world as possible.

Day 5: This is reserved for the true meth professionals because most people do not have the perseverance to stay up for 120 hours. In some instances, even if you keep up a constant drug intake, your body will just shut down on its own and induce sleep. It does take a special type of dedication to continue doing crystal at this stage. Craig and Justin were on day five.

They had run out of money and meth on day four and spent over twelve hours trying to scheme their next score. After countless phone calls their plans failed, and they became frustrated and aggravated by their lack of drugs. Craig blamed Justin for not having money, and Justin blamed Craig for not having drugs. The tension in the room was high, and they stopped talking to each other altogether.

A couple hours into their standoff, Craig spotted a tiny, individual crystal pebble under the coffee table. He just stared at it and came to the conclusion that a meth rock must have fallen to the ground in one of their line-cutting sessions.

Craig required a closer look, but he didn't want to alert Justin to his discovery with any sudden movements. He silently lowered himself off the couch and onto the floor.

Craig looked back at Justin, who was occupied with disassembling a CD Discman that recently stopped working. Craig knew this was the perfect distraction. He slowly extended his left arm under the table to grab the rock then slid it along the carpet until it was next to his hip pocket.

Craig examined the rock and knew it was too small for both of them to get high, so he made the executive decision to keep this his secret. In his heart, he knew Justin would do the same. He turned around one last time to ensure Justin hadn't gotten curious about his recent movements. Justin was clueless, preoccupied with the various parts of the Discman scattered all over the table.

Craig slid a tooter out of his pocket and eyeballed a razor blade on the table behind an ashtray. He grabbed the rock with his left hand and reached for the blade with his right. Within a few seconds, he transformed the rock into a miniature line. He scooped up the tooter and quickly leaned in toward the table. He was halfway through snorting the line when the silence was broken.

"You know you just snorted a Dorito, right?" Justin shouted from the kitchen.

Craig stopped mid-snort to investigate the remaining powder.

"You're a fucking liar," Craig said in frustration.
"Dude, I saw that shit yesterday, dumb fuck. I even tasted it—pretty sure it was Cool Ranch."

Craig did a numby to test the remaining powder.

"Yeah, it's Cool Ranch," he responded. He blew the remaining Dorito powder off the table.
"Fuck this shit! I need to get out of this fucking apartment," Justin said.
"Where?"
"Hopefully somewhere to get high."

Craig didn't want to stay in the apartment, but he was glued to the floor. Deep down he knew, especially after the Dorito incident, that he shouldn't be around another living soul that had slept in the last seventy-two hours. He watched as Justin put on his jacket and walk out the front door.

Justin ended up at Denny's in a booth by himself drinking coffee. The tables surrounding him were occupied by drunk people enjoying a late-night meal, attempting to sober up before the drive home.

He finished his coffee, paid the bill, and walked to the entrance. On his way out he spotted a stuffed-animal crane game. Justin pulled out his remaining two dollars and fed them into the machine. Unfortunately, both attempts came up empty.

"Fucking bullshit! Fuck that turtle!" He started to slam his head against the glass, drawing the attention of the staff. A brave young waiter approached Justin.
"Sir, I'm going to have to ask you to leave," the waiter politely said.
"Sure, no problem. I'm so sorry."

He left the restaurant, but on the walk to his car, he had a change of heart. He opened the passenger door, pulled a handgun out of the glove box, and gracefully strolled back into the Denny's.

The moment Justin re-entered the restaurant, the waiter who had just asked him to leave quickly approached. Justin revealed the gun, and the waiter retreated behind the counter and into the kitchen.

Justin stood in front of the game, took out the gun and banged it against the glass.

"Stupid fucking turtle!"

He took a step back then aimed the gun at the center of the glass.

BANG! BANG!

The glass shattered. Shrapnel flew throughout the restaurant and onto the lobby floor. Justin casually reached into the newly opened hole and retrieved the turtle. He cleaned off the shards of glass, placed it under his arm, turned around, and smiled.

"I had my eye on this little guy all night," he said and then calmly walked out of the restaurant and back to his car.

Justin then drove to a dance club located in a strip mall a few miles from Denny's. He fired a couple random shots into the windows, but the club was practically empty, so he missed everyone inside with his drive-by attempt.

Justin eluded the police for ten days, and on October 30th, 1995, he drove to his apartment complex. He parked across the street, and carefully surveyed the parking lot, searching for any sign of police activity. He concluded the coast was clear and cautiously walked to his apartment.

"Justin Cook! Get on the fucking ground and spread your legs!" a police officer shouted from the distance.

Justin grabbed the gun from his jacket and aimed in the officer's direction. He pulled the trigger and closed his eyes.

Nothing.

Justin pulled the trigger again, but again nothing happened. The gun malfunctioned, causing the bullet to jam in the chamber.

"Fuck! Fuck! Fuck!" Justin screamed.

Justin knew he had to act quickly to avoid any chance of getting shot. He threw the gun and simultaneously dropped like a corpse to the pavement below him. Within a few moments, he had a knee in his back and a gun to his head.

"Stay the fuck down! Don't fucking move, scumbag!"

He was handcuffed and escorted to the back of a police car, taking his last few breaths as a free, non-felon civilian.

In April of 1996, Justin was sentenced to thirteen years in the Colorado Department of Corrections for various charges, including theft less than $100 (for the stuffed turtle), third-degree burglary, and first-degree assault on a peace officer. That was the big one; it got him ten years. He was twenty-three.

I guess he could consider himself lucky; if the gun had fired, he would have gotten attempted murder or murder. I guess if you want to consider thirteen years in prison as luck.

....

Craig and I finally arrived at the parking lot and then wandered the endless lines of vehicles searching for my Dodge Dakota, the needle in a haystack in the maze of the Red Rocks parking lot. It's a difficult task in the daylight; with the sun setting, it was almost impossible. The drugs and booze did not help our navigation abilities either.

We finally located my truck right when there was an enormous eruption from the crowd; I knew White Zombie was taking the stage. I started calculating concert math in my head: they would get about a forty-five-minute set; if we hurried, it would take at least thirty-five minutes to reach the entrance. If we were lucky, we might see their last few songs.

"We're probably going to miss them," I said.
"Might as well get high then," Craig responded as he started preparing a foily.
"Just dump all of it," I suggested.
"Good call."

We sat in the bed of my truck, under the moonlit sky with music echoing through the canyon walls while we passed the tin foil back and forth.

About a half-mile hike and an hour later we were at the main gates. The line had vanished except for a few remaining bystanders. The security guard gave us a quick pat-down, tore our ticket stubs, and ushered us in. We ran to the tenth row, and pushed and elbowed our way to the center of the aisle.

"We are the fucking cowboys from hell," Craig yelled as the black curtain dropped onto the stage.

Wednesday, July 31st

I got home from the show around 3:00 a.m. and attempted to sleep, but I just lay there for hours, trying every sleeping trick I could think of. I lay on my back, and on my stomach; had music turned off, turned up, turned up really fucking loud; I counted sheep, but nothing worked. I even attempted to jerk off, but I couldn't get erect, so I just stared at the ceiling.

At around 6:00 a.m., I knew sleep wasn't coming anytime soon, so I decided to get up and plan out my day. I had just started scribbling random ideas in a notebook when I heard my mom walking down the stairs. I didn't want her to see me awake nor did I want to attempt talking to her, so I quickly climbed under the covers and pretended to be asleep.

There I was, a nineteen-year-old, pretending to be asleep to hide from my mom because I was strung out on meth. I was beginning to question my life choices at that point.

After she had retrieved some clothes from the dryer, she came into my room and stood above my bed.

"I love you," she whispered.

I lay motionless, waiting for her to leave. I contemplated telling her I was sorry, but I clenched my jaw like a steel trap so that I wouldn't say anything I'd regret. I remained in bed until I heard her walk out the front door, then I sat up. I didn't know if I should cry or do meth to forget this little incident. I decided to get high.

I staggered up the stairs to the living room and unscrewed a light bulb from one of the lamps. With the bulb in hand, I walked into the kitchen, opened a cabinet, and removed the toolbox. I rummaged inside the box until I found a pair of needle-nose pliers.

I sat down at the dining room table, pushed my mom's coffee cup aside, and started to go to work on the light bulb. I jammed the pliers into the base of the bulb then moved them back and forth, breaking the various wires and the inner mechanisms of the bulb. I dumped the broken fragments into the trash can and made my way to the sink to wash out the powder coating and anything else that remained in the bulb.

Then came the hardest part, waiting for the bulb to completely dry. I placed it upside down on the table and just watched as water drained down the sides of the glass. I quickly became impatient though and started blowing in the bulb to accelerate the drying process. When I deemed the process complete, I dropped a few rocks inside, inserted a tooter in the opening, and began smoking.

After five or six hits, I glanced up at the microwave. The clock displayed 8:27. I realized I was getting high alone before most people started their day, and I became disgusted with myself.

I dropped the bulb onto the kitchen floor and watched as it shattered into tiny glass pieces. I grabbed a broom from the closet and began sweeping up the glass. I shook my head as I guided the broom back and forth against the linoleum floor.

After I had cleaned up, I got ready and then drove to Tower Records. I walked up and down the aisles, flipping through piles and piles of CDs arranged by genre in alphabetical order. I approached the S's and stopped when a "New Release" sticker on a CD case caught my eye. I picked up the case and examined the artwork that had flowers surrounding a man's back tattoo with letters that spelled out "Sublime."

....

I really didn't know much about Sublime except I was supposed to see them play in February of 1996 at the Ogden Theater. On the night of the show, a group of us ended up drinking a lot. When I say "a lot," I mean shots of Jim Beam about every five minutes for an hour straight. Okay, I'm not sure if it was an hour, because I blacked out in under a half hour.

I remember being in a cheap hotel room with Mark, and then my next conscious memory was sitting in the backseat of Mark's car in a liquor store parking lot near the Ogden Theatre. I examined the vehicle: Mark was in the driver's seat, and there were two girls I didn't know, one sitting shotgun and the other next to me in the back. I was about to ask who they were when I felt an impending situation. I opened the door and started vomiting uncontrollably with such force that I could barely inhale. The Jim Beam and Subway mixture was hitting the pavement and splattering back into my face.

"He might have alcohol poisoning. Maybe we should take him to the hospital," one of the girls said to Mark.

I couldn't lift up my head, so I extended my middle finger then waved at them to leave me alone and go to the show.

"See, I told you he's fine. Let's go," Mark said.

I went from puking to sweating profusely to lying in the backseat to feeling better then back to starting the cruel cycle again. Finally, after twenty minutes of nothing coming out of my mouth I was convinced the incident was over.

I glanced into the rearview mirror and removed any vomit chunks remaining on my face and hair. I looked somewhat decent considering I was vomiting almost nonstop for about an hour.

I slapped myself in the face a few times, took a couple deep breaths, then opened the car door. I kicked my left foot out of the car with authority and placed it firmly on the ground, then my right foot. I pulled myself up with the coat hanger and placed my hand against the car door to gather my balance. I was starting to feel good about myself until I looked down. I was standing in a sea of

Jim Beam, Subway, bile, and blood. It was not a pretty picture; my shoes were almost completely covered.

My first instinct was to jump out of the puddle, but there was only one problem with that: In my intoxicated condition, my brain and body were not communicating on the same level. I attempted to jump out of the puddle of vomit but lost my footing and fell butt-first into my own puke puddle. I struggled to get out of the vomit before I began dry-heaving from the sight and smell.

I pulled myself up then leaned against Mark's car and started cleaning off the vomit that had accumulated on the back of my pants. Once I felt presentable, I started jogging toward the venue, stumbling most of the way.

I arrived at the corner of Colfax and Ogden with only a stoplight between me and my destination. I began frantically pressing the crosswalk button, and just before the walk sign changed, the front doors of the Ogden swung open and herds of sweaty concert-goers were exiting the venue. The show was over.

Less than three months after the show, on May 25th, 1996, the lead singer of Sublime, Bradley Nowell, overdosed on heroin and died. He was twenty-eight.

....

I figured if the lead singer OD'ed a few months after recording the album, it was worth my fourteen dollars. I purchased the CD and spent the rest of the afternoon running errands and consuming meth.

I was picking up Leah later that night, and my plan was to break up with her. I felt our relationship had run its course. I was tempted just to call or write a note, but I felt she deserved a face-to-face breakup.

I didn't have a legitimate reason to break up with her though and that's where I was running into a problem. I just wanted to fuck other girls, and I didn't want to feel guilty about it. I didn't think she would consider that a valid reason.

I rehearsed my speech all afternoon.

"Leah, I love you. I really do, but I think we should take a break. You're going back to school, and I'm working so much. I know we are never going to be able to see each other. I still want to be friends."

I prepared myself for yelling, tears, maybe even a few slaps or punches to the face. If I got away with only a couple bruises or scratches, I would consider that a victory.

My plan was to stay close to her house. I didn't want to break up with her then have to drive a long distance to drop her off. I wanted the least number of questions and crying on the return drive as possible.

I decided to go to a dirt parking lot on the top of Green Mountain a few minutes from her parents' house. Green Mountain is one of the highest peaks in the metro area, and you can see most of South Denver from the lot. Leah and I tripped acid there when we first started dating, and it seemed fitting to end our relationship there. It was a stunning view, especially after a few hits of acid.

I was nervous, so I just turned up the radio to avoid conversation. This was going to be the first time I broke up with a girl, and I wasn't looking forward to it. I mean, I broke up with a girl in sixth grade, but I don't count that one.

I parked my truck, and just stared at the city lights. My heart was racing, and I was having trouble swallowing. It was harder than I thought it was going to be.

She could sense something was wrong.

"I love you, baby," she whispered in my ear.

She then began kissing my neck and rubbing my crotch. I wanted to push her off me and tell her that we were finished, but it felt incredible, and I wasn't strong enough to stop her. Before I realized it, she had my pants unzipped and pulled out my dick. She leaned down between the steering wheel and my stomach and started giving me a blowjob. There was no possible way I could break up with her after receiving head.

"Hey Leah, thanks for giving me a blow job, but we are finished so get the fuck out. And sweetie, you still have some cum on your face."

I was an asshole, but not that big of an asshole. She got a stay of execution. I leaned back, closed my eyes, and hummed "Caress Me Down" by Sublime.

Saturday, August 10th

My vacation began on Monday the 5th, and it consisted of consuming meth nonstop for five days. I stayed at Mark's dealer's house so long it almost felt like a vacation home. I just traded in a beach and frozen drinks for a tweaker pad and tooters.

I was mostly snorting during the vacation, and I started to develop a love for it, well except for the drip. The drip occurs a few minutes after snorting a line. It is the meth slowly traveling down the nasal cavity into the throat while getting absorbed into the membranes of the nose and sinus cavities. Visualize sucking on a corroded 9-volt battery for a few minutes.

On that Thursday, my nose started bleeding uncontrollably, and I spent twenty minutes along with a roll of toilet paper cleaning up the blood. I was a mess. After the bleeding stopped, I investigated my nose in a mirror and saw the lining of my cartilage was becoming paper thin. I could feel a little hole starting to develop. It was time to switch from snorting to smoking, and time to trade my nose for my lungs.

On that Friday I left my tweaker vacation pad and went to my friend John's house, another guy I went to high school with. His mom was on a business trip, so it became our designated party house for the rest of the weekend. John was supposed to graduate in my class, but he got into a "little" trouble and was expelled from school. Well, maybe more than a little trouble.

During our junior year, a group of his computer friends illegally hacked into a long-distance company and accumulated about $30,000 in long distance charges downloading computer games from around the world. The FBI kicked in his front door and confiscated every piece of computer equipment in the house. The FBI thought they were planning a terrorist plot, but instead they were a bunch of high school kids who wanted to play video games.

Since they were all minors, the judge was lenient on them. They had to repay a portion of the phone charges, and they received one year of probation along with community service. That should have ended that situation, but not with John.

A few months later he broke into a local computer store where his friend worked. They ransacked the business and stole a few thousand dollars' worth of computer equipment. However, they forgot one minor detail: the store had video cameras, and they didn't wear masks.

This time, the judge was not so lenient on John. He was sentenced to six months in a halfway house on the weekends and house arrest during the week. A condition of this sentence was that he was required to remain enrolled in high school. If he dropped out, he would receive the full jail sentence. He performed like the model convict for a few months, but then he started sneaking acid in his textbooks during his weekend visits to the six-by-five jail cell that held only a bed, toilet, and sink.

A few months later, he dropped out of school and stopped going to the halfway house. He was picked up on a bench warrant and sentenced to the full fourteen months in the Jefferson County Jailhouse.

He was released in June of 1996, and it seemed like the simultaneous usage of drugs and jail time had an effect on his fragile mental state. He would have conversations with me about various ill-conceived plans that included drugs, computers, and breaking a magnitude of different state and federal laws. At one point, John spent hours trying to convince me to help him cook his first batch of meth, and even in my strung out state of mind, I knew it was a really, really bad idea.

I found the whole situation rather entertaining. If I had been newly introduced to John, I would have been worried, but I've known him since middle school, and he was mostly harmless.

"You guys want to smoke some crack?" he asked out of nowhere.

Jake, Craig, and I all looked up from our card game and nodded our heads.

I had done cocaine a few times since July, and I wasn't keen on it. I never understood why people preferred it over crystal. It was more expensive, it didn't last as long, and it didn't give you the high that meth does. Crack did pique my interest though. I'd never actually seen it except in those anti-drug PSA commercials from the 1980s featuring Pee Wee Herman.

This is crack, rock cocaine. It isn't glamorous, or cool, or kid stuff. It is the most addictive kind of cocaine, and it can kill you. What's really bad is nobody knows how much it takes, so every time you use it, you risk dying. It isn't worth it. Look, everybody wants to be cool, but doing it with crack isn't just wrong, it could be dead wrong.

I always wondered who was the fucking genius at the Drug Council that created that campaign and actually thought Pee Wee Herman and scary background music would stop kids from doing crack.

I was somewhat skeptical that John could produce crack at his dining room table, but once he started sorting various tools, I was convinced. Craig and I sat down and watched like we were students in a science classroom. His arsenal included cocaine, a lighter, baking soda, a glass of water, and rubbing alcohol.

"My uncle taught me how to prepare the ingredients to produce the perfect mixture."

He then spent the next half hour mixing, boiling, drying, and cooling the crack cocaine.

"And that is how you cook crack, boys!" John said with excitement as he displayed the final product.

On the table in front of us were four crack rocks ready to be smoked. John placed one into his crack pipe then took a hit and passed it to me. I lit the rock and inhaled an enormous cloud of crack-cocaine smoke. The rush was nothing I had ever experienced before, and I must admit it was pretty fucking intense. My only problem with it was that it didn't last very long. It was fun to try, but I still preferred crystal over crack and cocaine.

For the next few hours, people shuffled in and out of the house. We smoked meth, Jake cooked more batches of crack, and we played drinking games.

The party finally whittled down to John, Craig, Jake, and me. We were playing cards for hours when I looked at the clock and realized it was 3:00 a.m. My vacation ended in three hours. I knew I wasn't going to be able to sleep, but I needed to stop drinking and try to relax before work.

"I'm out, guys. I have to work in a couple hours. Good luck," I said as I threw my cards down.

I walked into the living room and turned down the lights, hoping to get my brain to shut off so that I could relax for a few hours. It worked for about ten minutes until I felt something I had never felt before … my heart beating.

BUMP, BUMP.

It's weird to explain, but if you can actually feel your heart beating, there's reason for concern. I sat up on the couch, and attempted to control my breathing.

BUMP, BUMP.

"Fuck!"

It felt like my heart was pounding out my chest. It was erratically bouncing back and forth against my rib cage like a pinball.

Overdosing was always a possibility, but the realization of it actually happening was terrifying.

I knew I couldn't call 911. There were so many drugs in the house that everyone would end up in jail. I wiped off the sweat that had accumulated on my forehead and rubbed my eyes, trying to clear up my vision.

"I am not going to die sitting on this fucking orange couch! No fucking way!" I said to myself.

I jumped off the couch and ran toward the patio door. I flung it open and stopped on the edge of the grass.

"This is good. This is good. I'm okay. It was just in my head."

BUMP, BUMP, BUMP.

The only solution I could conceive in my panicked state was to walk. It seemed that walking subdued the beating sensation. I started a combination of walking and running around the border of John's backyard. I completed one circle, then another and another. After finishing about ten of them, I stopped to check my heart.

BUMP, BUMP. BUMP, BUMP!

"Fuck!" I screamed as I started the run-walk pace again, drawing the attention of everyone at the table playing cards. Jake and Craig walked outside.

"What the hell are you doing?" Jake asked.
"Go back inside. I just needed some air." I could barely get the words out without my voice cracking.

Craig ran across the yard to catch up with me.

"Dude, it's almost four in the morning, and you're running around the backyard like a fucking crazy person."

I stopped walking, grabbed his hand and put it on my chest.

"Feel that? I think I'm overdosing."
"I do feel something. I feel a pussy who can't handle his drugs,"
Craig said as he started laughing.

I did not find his comment humorous.

"Dude, you're fine. Just come back inside," Jake yelled from a lawn
chair.
"Fuck you guys! I can't stop walking!" I said to them with a death
stare.

I continued my path around the grass border of the backyard with
my head down, focusing on every upcoming step. Craig and Jake
sat on the patio furniture to keep me company. They cheered me
on with the first few passes until they got bored and returned
inside.

I stopped after counting about 100 trips around the backyard. I was
positive I couldn't walk anymore. My legs were starting to shake,
and they felt like Jell-O.

I stood there, anticipating the heart-beating sensation to return. It
didn't.

I went back inside and took up residence on the orange couch and
closed my eyes. The time was 5:15 a.m., and I had to work in forty-
five minutes.

Sunday, August 11th

I contemplated calling in sick, but I was on the verge of getting fired for multiple write-ups—I stopped counting at eleven. In the spring of 1996, management caught Jake and me smoking weed on our break and fired us, but they didn't follow proper union protocol and were required to reinstate our jobs. Jake quit the next day, and I continued working there. It wasn't an ideal work environment because management was looking for any reason to fire me. I knew a fireable reason would be calling in sick less than an hour before my scheduled shift.

It was a struggle, but I completed the first four hours. I clocked out for lunch and drove home with every intention of getting fifteen minutes of rest. I walked into the kitchen, and there was a note my mom had left on the table.

Went to Church, be back around noon. There are donuts on the counter. Love Mom.

I stared at the donuts then put the note in my pocket and walked downstairs to my bedroom. Craig was sitting on a recliner preparing a line. He had gotten kicked out of his parents' house and was splitting time between Jake's house and mine. Unfortunately for me, he was at my house that morning.

"Dude, put that shit away. I need to rest for a few minutes." I said to him.
"Are you fucking crazy? If you lay down right now, you're going to be out for hours if not days. You might as well come over here and join me so you can get through the last few hours of work."

He was right. If I closed my eyes, I would probably not wake up until Monday afternoon. I calculated that if I snorted a decent sized line, I would get high enough to finish work, and I could crash the moment I got home.

"Fine, give it here," I said to him.

....

I returned to work at 11:00 a.m., and every register was open with a line of shopping carts behind it. The store was filled with beeps from registers, customers asking questions about coupons, and babies crying. I decided on register fifteen.

"Paper or plastic?" I asked the woman in her mid-forties.
"Plastic is fine."

I started the routine I had done thousands of times. I put my head down and placed eggs, bread, potato chips, and countless other items in various bags. I was about halfway finished with the order when a bead of sweat fell onto the metal platform below.

I felt my forehead, and it was drenched. I knew I didn't look presentable, so I lowered my forehead as far as possible, trying to hide my current condition from the customer and cashier.

I was focusing on the items coming down the conveyor belt when I started to lose my vision. My window of visibility just kept getting smaller and smaller until I could only see about four inches wide by two inches high directly in front of my face. Everything outside that rectangle was pitch-black.

While my vision was fading, I failed to notice that my hearing was completely gone—no intercom pages, customer small talk, or awful seventies music over the public address system. For some reason, the hearing didn't worry me as much as the vision did. Under normal circumstances, going deaf would be cause for panic, but not at that moment. My vision was my top priority.

I wanted to start cursing Craig for getting me high.

My plan was to finish the order then walk outside or to the water fountain to regroup. I started grabbing blindly for anything that was

57

traveling down the conveyor belt, placing whatever I could reach into the closest grocery bag. When I could no longer feel anything, I assumed the order was complete, smiled in the direction of the customer, and turned around.

To my left was the front entrance and the safety of Sunday afternoon sunlight. I would have to maneuver past fourteen other registers all while navigating through customers, random shopping carts, and kids waiting to saddle up on the penny horse ride.

To my right were five registers and a water fountain that was about 100 feet straight ahead. I knew if I could make it there, I could splash water on my face and try to regain my senses. Going right seemed like the logical decision.

I started taking baby steps with my hand extended out in front of my body until I reached the back wall. I turned right and began the slow journey to my destination using the back wall as a guide. After a few minutes, I finally made it to the water fountain; it was one of my proudest moments in recent memory. I felt like I had reached the summit of Mount Evans.

I searched the fountain until I located the round metal button. I pressed it, dipped my face into the water stream, and started drinking as fast as I could. The cool water on my forehead felt calming, and for a moment I forgot I was temporarily deaf and blind.

As I was standing there contemplating my next move, my vision returned as fast as it went away, and after about a minute it was back to 100 percent. I was relieved but still missing one important sense.

I plugged my nose, closed my mouth and eyes, then forced air out my ears until I heard a pop. My hearing had finally returned, and I could faintly hear "Paint it Black" by The Rolling Stones playing over the PA. A song about a death and the funeral procession seemed fitting.

Saturday, August 17th

I spent a week loathing the idea of going into work. I wasn't sure if I was embarrassed about what happened, or if I was worried that it might happen again. Either way, I dreaded every time I walked through the front entrance.

I knew I couldn't suffer through another shift, so after three years of employment, I decided to quit. I had always envisioned the moment in my head and had rehearsed it time and time again. I would walk up to the manager's desk, throw my red apron at a manager, tell them I hope they die, then walk away with both middle fingers raised to the ceiling.

I opted for a simple phone call instead.

"This is Scott. I quit."

The real-life version was not as dramatic.

I felt a celebration was in order. I made the appropriate phone calls and was out of the house by noon to pick up Leah, Craig, Mark, and Tony. I was over our normal drug locations, so we decided to go to downtown Denver and 16th Street mall.

The 16th Street Mall is a pedestrian sidewalk in the heart of downtown Denver lined with shops, restaurants, bars, and skyscrapers on both sides of the street. The streets are full of tourists, business workers and homeless kids begging for money or cigarettes.

There is also a large number of street performers on about every corner who may or may not be homeless. Most of the performers are musicians playing some version of a cover with a guitar case open for the tips. The majority of them couldn't play two chords, but on a rare occasion there would be a guy who could play brilliantly. When I stumbled across that, I would dig into my pocket and toss whatever change I had into the guitar case. It was good, but not good enough for paper money.

We walked the mall for an hour until we came to the consensus that it was time to get high. The only problem was that downtown Denver on a beautiful summer Saturday afternoon does not provide many opportunities for smoking crystal meth.

Mark and I ventured into an alley and stopped behind a dumpster. I looked up the alley then back to the street.

"This looks good, right?" Mark asked.
"I think this is about as safe as it's going to get."

We crouched down behind the dumpster and were about to light up when a dishwasher walked out of a restaurant back door with a trash bag about ten feet from us. Mark quickly slipped the light bulb into his backpack.

"That was a fucking close call," I whispered as we quickly walked out of the alley.

We walked around for the next half hour scouring the Denver streets for any place that would be suitable to get high. I was about to give up when Craig found a location he deemed appropriate.

"This is perfect!" Craig shouted with excitement.

Craig's perfect location was Trinity United Methodist Church on Broadway a few blocks north of the state capital. The church had a stairwell on the side of the building that was hidden from the street and could provide us enough cover to smoke.

I was reluctant to smoke meth on the grounds of a church.

"Isn't this a little sacrilegious?" I asked.
"No. Just say a little prayer before you take a hit," he responded.

I just stared at him.

"It's a verse in the Bible. Steve 4:14, I believe."
"You're a fucking idiot," I retorted.

Mark and I walked down the stairs while everyone else became a lookout at street level.

When we reached the bottom of the steps, Mark removed all the smoking materials required. While he was emptying his backpack, he dropped a baggie of meth onto the ground, and I quickly reached down to retrieve it.

Mark offered me first hit, but I refused. He instantly took that as his invitation. I dejectedly watched as Mark took the hit and then exhaled the white crystal smoke on the burgundy brick walls of the church.

I couldn't believe we had come to this. The church had been there for over a hundred years; people got baptized there, got married there, had funerals there, and celebrated life and death there.

"Are you okay with this?" I asked Mark.
"Yeah, this shit is fucking good," he said while he coughed out the remnants of his hit.
"No, that's not what I'm talking about."
"Then what the fuck are you talking about?"
"Nevermind!"

Thursday, August 22nd

My dad was pissed after I quit, and he threatened to kick me out of the house unless I had a job before the end of the month. I had to figure out something fast because I didn't want to spend my savings on rent in some shitty, run-down apartment.

My mom knew a lady who was a regional manager of a sporting goods store, and she was looking to hire people at their brand new store in the yet-to-be opened Park Meadows mall.

The upscale mall was located in southeast Denver in an affluent part of town. I wasn't looking forward to the thirty-minute drive so that I could work with people I knew I would hate and customers I would hate more. I also had zero desire to work in retail again, but this was a job and enough to satisfy my dad, allowing me to continue to live at home for free.

My mom set up an interview for Craig and me, and we were hired on the spot.

"Can you start today?" the hiring manager asked.

I wanted to tell her no because I had plans to get high that afternoon, but I figured that might be frowned upon.

"Of course! I can't wait to join the team," I said.
"Sure." Craig did not share my fake enthusiasm.

The mall grand opening was scheduled a week after we started, and the store was nowhere close to being finished. The shelves were empty, and the store was in disarray. I think the only reason they hired us was that we spoke English and had a pulse. I spent the first four days removing shirts from boxes, tagging them, putting them on hangers then placing them on different racks. Small, medium and large; blue, red, orange, green and black. Over and over and over again.

"Keep up the amazing, hard work! With that pace, we'll be ready for the grand opening!" a manager said with an ear-to-ear grin.

I wanted to turn around and punch him in the dick.

On our fifth day of work, I was immediately thrown into a group of about ten other employees. We began role-playing exercises on how to sell the proper running shoe. I felt like fucking Al Bundy.

I had made a promise to myself to be a good employee and not get high while I was on the clock, but the role-playing put me over the edge. I knew I couldn't keep that promise after four hours of pretending to sell women's athletic shoes.

I searched the store until I found Craig fucking around on the loading dock doing his best to avoid any real work.

"Do you have anything?" I whispered to him.
"You know it," he happily responded.

We clocked out for lunch and began exploring the newly completed mall that had an aroma of wet paint and freshly laid drywall. Construction workers were on every corner making the finishing touches. We entered a hallway that was a maze of twists and turns that connected various stores. We finally found a secluded corner that was a perfect location to get high.

Craig started to remove the supplies from his pants pocket when I heard footsteps coming down the hall. I grabbed Craig's hand and pushed it back into his pocket just as a construction worker turned the corner.

"Oh sorry, guys, just need to fix the light," he said in an embarrassed tone as he looked away.

I looked down and realized my hand was still in Craig's pocket. He probably thought I was about to give Craig a hand job when he interrupted the two of us. I removed my hand and started walking in the opposite direction with Craig right behind me.

"Fuck this fucking job! I'm done," I said.
"My thoughts exactly."

I ripped off my name tag and threw it on the cement, and we pushed open a door to the outside parking lot.

Monday, August 26th

I was parked at the Lakewood Police Department staring at my stereo clock. It was 9:30 a.m. I had court in thirty minutes for the minor-in-possession ticket I received in July.

I was doing my best to calculate my entrance exactly so that I would have to spend the least amount of time in the courtroom as possible. I didn't want to be late, but I sure as shit did not want to be early. I didn't want to sit and listen to some fucking judge talk about bullshit for any longer than I had too.

That was the second time I was ever in front of a judge. The first time was when I was fifteen, and I got caught smashing mailboxes with John and a few other friends. The judge sentenced me to ten hours of community service and ordered that I return for the next three months to report my progress to him. I skipped the third month, and he threatened me with time in a juvenile detention center. In the end, he added three additional months and ten hours onto my sentence.

Over the course of those six months, I spent twenty hours in a church basement stapling the weekly church newsletter together. I despised every minute and would have done anything to avoid the punishment of community service again.

I strolled into the courtroom a few minutes early. Jake, Mark, and Andre were already there, spread out sporadically throughout the courtroom. A few days before court, we conceived a plan to avoid each other in an attempt to trick the judge into thinking that we were not friends in hopes of receiving a lighter sentence. I took it as far as avoiding eye contact with all of them.

I also thought I would get off easier than the rest of them because I only had the mailbox incident on my record. I was practically clean compared to the rest of them.

Mark had the most extensive criminal record of all of us. It included a drug offense, trespassing, and third-degree sexual assault. The sexual assault happened when Mark was drunk at Southwest Plaza and grabbed some random girl's ass. He was arrested a short time later in the arcade, and after the cops had him handcuffed, he started begging them to shoot him in the head. They didn't listen to his request and booked him with the sexual assault along with a consumption ticket.

One night in the spring of 1996, Jake, Andre, myself along with a few other people were driving home from Lookout Mountain after a night of drinking and smoking pot. Jake got pulled over on C470 for doing 87 in a 55. He was taking the roadside sobriety test, when the backup officer discovered a five-foot bong in the trunk. That was the nail in the coffin. Jake received a DUI, but the cop let the drug paraphernalia ticket slide.

Andre's criminal record included a drug-possession ticket, another consumption ticket as well as a few speeding tickets.

Jake went first, and after the charges were read, the judge lectured him about the evils of drinking alcohol and how it could ruin any aspirations and dreams that Jake had for the future. After the lecture, he gave him six months' probation, twenty-five hours of community service, a $100 fine, and required him to attend one alcohol class.

Andre was next, and he received the same sentence. Mark casually strolled up to the podium, and his outcome was the same as the others.

The bailiff finally called my name. I stood up and adjusted my tie and dress shirt then walked up to the podium. I was doing my best to avoid eye contact with the judge. He read my charges then looked directly at me.

"Do you still drink, Scott?" he asked in his authoritative, judge-sounding voice.

"Your Honor, that was one of the first times I drank, and I have not done it since. I guess you could say it scared me away from drinking."

"That is a smart decision, son. Alcohol will send you down a dark and negative path. I wish you all the luck. Your sentence is six months probation, twenty-five hours of community service, a $100 fine, and you are required to attend one alcohol education class."

That motherfucking cocksucker!

"Thank you, your honor," I said as I turned away.

Friday, August 30th

I had tickets to see The Smashing Pumpkins at McNichols Sports Arena. A few weeks before the show I was unsure if it would actually happen.

The Smashing Pumpkins released the double album *Mellon Collie and the Infinite Sadness* in the fall of 1995, and it was an immediate success. The album debuted at number one on the Billboard 200, sold over one million copies in the first week, and produced six singles.

They embarked on a World Tour in the winter of 1996. It started in Toronto then they spent the next six months crisscrossing the globe, making their way to Japan, Australia, Europe, and finally back to the US. They played random cities over the next few weeks until they arrived in New York City on July 11th. They were scheduled to play the first of two sold-out shows at Madison Square Garden the following night.

In the early-morning hours of July 12th, Jimmy Chamberlain, the drummer of the Smashing Pumpkins called 911 from his hotel room at the Regency Hotel on Park Avenue. He told them that his friend and touring keyboardist Jonathan Melvoin was unresponsive on the floor of his hotel room. They allegedly advised Jimmy to put Melvoin's head in the shower in an attempt to revive him until paramedics arrived. Once the paramedics arrived at the scene, they made several attempts to revive him, but Jonathan was pronounced dead at the scene. He died from a mixture of alcohol and a lethal strain of heroin known as Red Rum. He was thirty-four.

The remaining members of the Smashing Pumpkins kicked Jimmy out of the band, canceled the two MSG shows, and postponed the tour until they could find adequate replacements. The tour resumed on August 28th in Las Vegas, then went on to Salt Lake City, and finally to Denver on the 30th.

You would think that a member of a band whom I idolized and who overdosed and died would have an effect on me, but for some reason it didn't. I just did my best to convince myself that it was his time to go. It couldn't happen to me; it wouldn't happen to me.

As I walked into the arena, the opening piano melody of "Mellon Collie and The Infinite Sadness" echoed throughout the concourse.

Saturday, September 7th

My brother got married in the summer of 1995 to a girl of Mexican descent, and they had the wedding at a tiny church in central Denver. My nephew was getting baptized there.

The church was located in what would best be described as a barrio. The neighborhood was a low poverty area with homes that were in shambles, vehicles parked on cinder blocks in the front yards, and street vendors selling ice cream products from a cart with a bell that rang constantly.

"Helado! Helado!"

I got the impression it had a higher crime rate than neighborhoods I was accustomed to. I bet if I would have knocked on ten doors, I probably could have scored drugs from five of them.

I convinced Craig to come to the baptism with me by telling him there would be some fuckable girls there. It was a lie, but he bought it.

We left my house twenty minutes before the baptism was scheduled to start, and the drive was at least twenty-five minutes away. I was speeding in and out of traffic, running through yellow lights and stop signs, trying to avoid being tardy. The last thing I wanted was to be late for my nephew's baptism.

I was in the middle of a two-day bender and knew there was no way I could properly function without being high. I was having issues tying my shoes, so having conversations with family members would be a problem. Before we left, I dumped an excessive amount of crystal in a light bulb, intending to smoke it all on the drive to the church.

Craig had taken the first hit before we reached the end of the block. He took three more hits before it was my turn—the customary process of driving while getting high. Craig then lit the flame and maneuvered the smoke filled bulb and tooter toward my mouth. Without taking my eyes off the road, I located the tooter with my lips and inhaled the smoke.

We repeated this process until the bulb was cashed, a block away from the church. I looked down at the clock, and somehow I managed to pull into the parking lot minutes before the scheduled starting time.

We ran into the church and quickly sat down in a pew next to my parents and other family members. I began worrying that someone might be able to smell the meth smoke on our clothes, but those thoughts quickly vanished when I realized that if someone could smell us, they either wouldn't know what it was or were users themselves. In all reality, we smelled more like the exhaust of a school bus than having just had a meth hot-box session.

I looked up as the priest began to speak.

"Hello, I would like to welcome you all here today for this happy and joyous occasion. We are here to celebrate and baptize our sons, our daughters, our grandchildren, our nephews and nieces, and friends and family."

He then paused for a moment and began talking again, but this time in Spanish. Craig leaned over to me.

"What the fuck is going on?" he whispered out the side of his mouth.

In our rush to get seated, I didn't notice the church was full of Mexican families. I estimated that there was a total of eight families, and we were the only white group in the building and probably the only family that spoke fluent English.

The priest transitioned back to English and then to Spanish again. After he had done this four or five times in a few minutes, Craig again leaned toward me and whispered.

"I am freaking the fuck out. I need to get the fuck out of here," he said in what he thought was a quiet, library voice.

The elderly Spanish lady seated in front of us overheard him and turned around to shake her head in a disapproving manner.

I agreed with Craig. It took every ounce of willpower not to lose my shit. I felt like I was involved in some sort of exorcism. When you're high on meth, there are many places you want to avoid—being in a Mexican church where the priest speaks both English and Spanish is high on that long list. It seemed like the beginning scene of a horror movie.

I just closed my eyes and imagined I was having a threesome with the two hot Mexican girls who were sitting across the aisle from me.

Friday, September 13th

I was standing in line at the top of Red Rocks about fifteen people back from the main gate. This was the final Red Rocks show of the season. I went to Bush, No Doubt, Goo Goo Dolls, Warped Tour, 311, White Zombie, Pantera, and probably a few others I can't remember, but this show was the one I was looking forward to the most: Rage Against the Machine.

They released their second album, *Evil Empire* in April of 1996, and it reached number one on the Billboard 200. Almost every time I turned on the radio, a song from the album was being played; it was the soundtrack to our summer. The local rock station, KBPI, sponsored the show and put the tickets on sale for $12.70. The 9,000-seat venue sold out within minutes.

Under normal circumstances, I would have been in the parking lot getting intoxicated and not waiting in line, but I had ulterior motives for being in there early.

The night before the show, Mark and I parked in the top lot of Red Rocks and started the walk down the path. After a few minutes, we reached the summit. Seventy rows below was the stage.

It's a spectacular view, especially at 3:00 a.m. with the moon as the only source of light. I stopped for a moment to take it all in. The downtown Denver skyline is visible about twenty miles to the east. The amphitheater is surrounded by two enormous red-rock formations that rise hundreds of feet into the sky, creating the perfect acoustic setting. The rocks formed over 200 million years ago and were there when dinosaurs walked the Earth. The fucking dinosaurs! A T-Rex could have been in my exact position. Breathtaking moments like that made me appreciate life.

The appreciation was short-lived.

We jogged down about forty rows until I found what I was looking for. "Here it is," I said to Mark as I pointed to an evergreen.

I had discovered this tree at the previous show and deemed it suitable to stash contraband. I removed a plastic bullet from my pocket and placed it in a tiny hole in the tree.

A bullet is a small device that allows you to do powder on the go without the hassle of cutting out lines. The intended purpose is for tobacco, but who the fuck are we kidding—it's primary used for illegal powders. A bullet has a container that houses the powder, a twist valve, and a chamber. When you're ready to snort, you turn the valve to fill up the chamber then turn it back to snort a premeasured amount of powder.

My plan was to retrieve it immediately after I got admitted into the show. The hole was large enough to hold the bullet but small enough to avoid security's radar when they checked for drug paraphernalia. It was a gamble stashing it there, but I would rather risk losing the coke in a tree than having a security guard discover it on me during the pat-down.

I anxiously waited for the gates to open, looking at the time on my pager about every thirty seconds hoping that would expedite the process.

The gates finally opened, and within five minutes it was my turn to enter. I had all my personal items in hand to accelerate the pat-down process. The overweight, middle-aged guard practically gave me a full body cavity search. I was ecstatic that I had hidden the bullet instead of trying to sneak it past that asshole. He finally ushered me inside the gate, and I handed my ticket to the next worker in line.

It was now a mad dash to the tree and the drugs. I was weaving in and out of the crowd, but had to stop about half way up to catch my breath because it was the most I had run in years. I should have stretched. I re-started my sprint up the last twenty rows, a little slower and less intense.

When I finally arrived at the tree, I almost passed out from exhaustion. I leaned against it until I caught my breath then looked in both directions to ensure no one was watching. I slowly reached into the hole and felt a tiny piece of plastic—the bullet.

"A bullet in my motherfucking head!"

Saturday, September 14ᵗʰ

I woke up to the news that Tupac Shakur died in Las Vegas from multiple gun shots that he received in a drive-by shooting after the Mike Tyson fight in Las Vegas. He was twenty-five.

I watched CNN until I finally decided to turn off the TV. I was becoming consumed by the coverage and needed something to distract me or I would watch reports on his death for hours.

I grabbed the cordless phone and started paging everyone I could think of. My parents were on a vacation to North Dakota, and I wanted to have a party. I patiently waited for the phone to ring. Once it did, I began to put together a game plan for the night.

I spent the remainder of the day gathering supplies for the festivities: two cases of PBR, a bottle of cheap vodka, and an 8-ball of meth. I figured this should be enough to suffice everyone that I invited, about ten people.

....

The first few hours of the night were rather uneventful and boring. Mark was igniting a new foily every twenty minutes like clockwork. Andre was arguing about music, Craig was in the spare bedroom fucking some girl, and Leah was annoying the shit out of me.

If I thought I could have operated a vehicle, I would have driven her to the closest bus stop, but since that wasn't possible, I just walked away from her every time she opened her mouth to talk to me. That had been the blueprint for the last few months: drink, get high, fight, fuck, and repeat. I needed a change.

Around 11:30 Jake finally walked through the front door with Samantha, and her friend. She was stunning. She was about five one and petite, and had long blonde hair and the biggest tits I'd ever seen. The moment that she walked in I knew I was going to try my hardest to fuck her.

I glanced back to the patio and saw that Leah was smoking a cigarette with Mark. He was talking nonstop to her, high as fuck, so she was going to be occupied for some time, giving me the opportunity to properly introduce myself to Samantha's friend.

I casually walked over to the group and gave Jake a high five then hugged Samantha. I then focused my attention on the friend.

"Hey, I'm Scott. I live here," I said.
"I'm Claire," she responded as she started to extend her hand toward me. I moved her hand aside and gave her a hug.
"Brother's gotta hug!" I quickly responded with a quote from *Tommy Boy*.
"Okay," she said while giggling.

The four of us made small talk for a few minutes before I interrupted the chit chat.

"Hey Claire, do you want a tour of the house?"
"Ok, I guess."

The girl had zero personality, but every time I looked down at her chest, I ignored her lack of conversation skills.

I grabbed her hand and guided her throughout the rooms of the house until we reached the final destination of the tour: the master bathroom. I removed a baggie of crystal from my pocket and began cutting up two lines on the countertop. The look on her face told me that she had never seen powder before.

"Are you cool with this?" I asked.
"Is that cocaine?"
"No, no, no… this is crystal meth, better than coke."
"Um, I don't know. I have never done that stuff before."
"It's awesome. You'll love it. I pinky swear." I said as I offered up

my pinky finger.
"Pinky swear?" she asked.
"Yes!"

We entwined our pinkies as I handed her a tooter. I then offered up some last-minute advice.

"It might burn your nostrils a little, so start off slow. You don't have to do the whole thing in one try."

She leaned over the bathroom counter, I did a countdown, and then I leaned against the wall and watched as she bent over and snorted the line.

She instantly sprang back up and then stood there like a statue for a few moments with her eyes closed and her mouth open. I waited for any type of reaction. She finally began to smile.

"That was fucking awesome! Can I do another one?" she eagerly asked.

I graciously offered it up and watched in delight as she did the second line. In my opinion, there's nothing hotter than watching an incredibly stunning girl snort crystal meth. I just wanted to pull my cock out and ask her to start sucking it, but I figured that was a little premature at that point.

We had been gone for a half hour, and I knew I was pushing my luck with Leah. Sooner or later she would come looking for me, and I would have to explain why Claire and I were alone in the bathroom doing crystal. I quickly manufactured a little white lie.

"I need to go into the bedroom and make a call. You can go downstairs and hang out with everyone in the kitchen. Cool?"
"You are going to come down there, right?" she asked.
"Yeah, I just need to make this call."
"Okay, see you in a minute."

I watched her walk out of the master bathroom, and then I closed the door behind her. I knew if I played my cards right, I could easily fuck her. I just needed to figure how to overcome the only obstacle, Leah. I stared at myself in the mirror, trying to come up with any feasible way to accomplish my plan.

"I could drive Leah home. No, I'm too fucked up to drive. That is out of the question. What about sending her out on a cigarette run? No, that wouldn't be enough time. Fuck. Think Scott, think," I said as I started banging my head with the palm of my hand.

I paused for a moment and lowered my head.

BANG, BANG.

"Scott! I don't feel ... good," Leah said, as she hiccupped.

I opened the door, and Leah was standing in the hallway, swaying back and forth with her eyes barely open.

"Fuck! Leah, are you okay?" I said as I placed my hands around her waist.
"I drank a lot."
"Yeah, it looks like it."

I picked her up, carried her into the bedroom, and placed her head on a pillow.

"I'm sorry," she said.
"It's okay, don't be sorry."
"Do you love me?"
"Of course," I responded.

We sat in silence until she passed out. I remained on the bed for another twenty minutes then gave her a kiss on the forehead, and turned off the light.

....

I went downstairs and joined the rest of the party. We spent the next few hours doing meth, drinking beers, and doing shots. Some people left, some people passed out, and some people disappeared. Around 3:30 a.m. I was finally alone with Claire in my bedroom.

I decided that was as good a time as any and moved in for a kiss. She pulled away from my lips.

"What are you doing? I thought Leah was your girlfriend?"
"No, she's—"
"She's not? That's not what I heard!"
"Let me explain. I've broken up with her numerous times, but she always says we can work it out. I don't want to be with her anymore."

I slowly looked up at her with puppy eyes, hoping she would believe the bullshit I was stringing together. There was a long silence.

"Do you promise? I don't want to be one of those girls that breaks up a relationship."

I held my hand up and extended my pinky finger.

"I pinky swear."

She laughed and then leaned toward me, and we started kissing. We continued with foreplay until I had her completely naked on my bed.

I knew after I fed her a few lines I would be in this situation. Meth is an aphrodisiac and pushes sex drive to the highest level. To cut to the chase, people want to fuck when they're high on crystal. Fucking her was inevitable, like a ticking time bomb. 3 ... 2 ... 1 ...

"Do you have a condom?" she asked moments before I was about to insert my penis inside of her.
"Of course."

That was a complete, fucking lie. I hadn't used a condom since I lost my virginity.

I leaned over and opened my nightstand drawer. I rummaged around in it until I found what I was looking for, a KitKat candy bar. I knew opening the KitKat would emulate the sound of a condom wrapper opening. I tore open the plastic, pretended to put the condom on, then bent her over on my bed and placed my cock inside her. She let out a soft moan.

Game, set, and match.

After we finished, we cuddled in my bed until Samantha walked into the room.

"Claire, we have to go! My parents are going to wake up soon," Samantha whispered.

Claire got dressed, we said our goodbyes, and Claire, Samantha and Jake left.

I went upstairs to the bedroom where Leah was still passed out. I stood in the doorway and began to feel guilty. That was the first time I ever cheated on a girlfriend, and it was not a pleasant feeling.

"Fuck." I whispered as I climbed into bed next to Leah.

Tuesday, September 17th

I parked a few houses down from Leah's parents' house. This was going to be the day I was going to break up with her. It was something that was months in the making, and I also felt bad about fucking Claire that night—then three days later, then a few days after that.

I had a plastic grocery bag filled with Leah's belongings that I accumulated over the course of our relationship. There were a couple hoodies, a pair of pants, a few bras, and a Green Day T-shirt that she stole from Spencer Gifts.

I failed miserably at the face-to-face breakup, so I attempted to do it over the phone but retracted when she started crying. I decided that dropping off a bag with a "we are over" note tied to it was the best way to end our ten-month relationship.

I slowly crept my way up the street, still unsure if I wanted to break up with her. I went back and forth about twenty-five times on the way to her house. I finally reached her driveway and parked.

"Fuck it! I'll be able to get her back if I want," I said.

I jumped out of my truck, ran to the front door, dropped the bag, knocked on the door, and ran away. I had no idea why I knocked. I guess it reminded me of my ding dong ditching days. As I was driving away, Leah opened the door and waved.

That was the last time I saw Leah.

I pulled my pager out of my pocket, turned it off, then threw it onto the passenger floor. I knew she was going to start blowing me up, and I didn't want to hear the constant buzzing.

I still had a few hours left until I had my court-ordered alcohol education class from the MIP ticket that I got in July. I thought about driving around until the class started, but I decided to return home and pray Leah didn't show up and cause a scene.

The more I thought about the class, the more upset I got about it. It was going to cost forty dollars to listen to some asshole—who probably had never sipped alcohol—lecture for two hours about the consequences of drinking. I contemplated skipping it until I remembered that would result in a bench warrant.

I arrived home with the best intentions of just relaxing until I had to leave, but it didn't work out that way. Craig was sitting on the couch about to snort a line.

"Wanna join?" Craig said as he offered the CD case.
"Dude, I have to go to an alcohol class in an hour, and you want me to get high?"
"It's an alcohol class, not a drug class. Two big differences."
"Fuck you. I don't think that is how it works," I said as I laughed.
"Have you ever been to one of these classes?"
"No."
"Well, trust me. They're boring as fuck. Getting high will make it more entertaining, and I bet you pay attention and maybe even learn a few things."
"Fuck, give it here!"

....

An accident turned my drive to the police station from thirty minutes to fifty-five. I pulled into a parking spot at 5:56 p.m. and the class started at 6:00. I ran across the parking lot and approached a stairwell. I was jumping five stairs at a time and cleared the complete staircase in six leaps. Caught up in my efforts to land each jump, I hadn't glanced up to notice the group of cops assembled at the bottom of the stairs.

I completely startled them, and they all took a few steps back. One cop put his hand on his holster. I stopped dead in my tracks.

"Sorry," I said as I cautiously walked around them.

I was so high I didn't even realize how fast I was running or how much noise I was making. I imagined the cops thinking I was a group of escaped convicts running down the stairs. It must have scared the shit out of them, and I was probably a few seconds from serious consequences.

I arrived in the classroom with one minute to spare, signed in, and took a seat in the last remaining desk in the second row. The instructor began his introduction and asked a question.

"Could someone tell me something that they've done while drunk that they've regretted?"

My hand instantly shot up.

Fall 1996

Wednesday, September 25th

"Dude, pick me up in an hour at my parents' place. I have some good news," Mark said with excitement.

"What is it?"

"It's a secret! See you in an hour," he said as he hung up.

My brain ran the gamut of what Mark wanted to tell me—it could have been anything from him winning five dollars on a scratch ticket to him finding an ounce of crystal. I decided it would be best not to try to get inside Mark's mind because that was a dangerous place, so I just stopped thinking about it.

I took a shower and smoked a personal-sized foily. I equated doing a morning foily with someone who needs a cup of coffee in the morning when they wake up. They served the same purpose only mine was illegal, destroyed my mind and body, and had a little more of a kick.

I arrived to pick up Mark five minutes early. It never failed; even if I did my best to be late, I would always arrive early. The worst part about being early was that Mark was always late. That never failed either. I waited anywhere from a half hour to almost two hours. That was his record.

After about twenty minutes, I got antsy. "Fuck this shit," I said as I turned on my truck.

I drove three blocks and parked directly in front of his house. Just as I was about to exit my vehicle, the front door flew open with Mark leaping out it. He was running full speed toward me with a duffle bag over his shoulder.

Mark's mother appeared in the doorway wearing a bathrobe and bedroom slippers, and holding an aluminum Louisville Slugger baseball bat.

"Get back in this house right now, Mark!" she yelled at him with an insane stare in her eyes.

Mark didn't look back and continued the sprint. He flung the duffel bag in the bed of my truck without interrupting his stride and continued to the passenger side door. He got in and instantly locked the door behind him.

"What the fuck is going on?"
"I would suggest you drive because she will beat the fuck out of your truck if you don't," he said, pointing back at his mom.

I turned around, and his mom was now running down the driveway with one slipper missing. I pulled down the gear shifter and stomped on the gas. I looked into the rearview mirror, and she was jumping up and down like a cartoon character in the middle of the street. I turned the corner, and she disappeared from view.

"I would suggest you don't park your car anywhere close to your house tonight because she's going to be looking for me and your truck all night long," he said like nothing happened.
"Why was she chasing you with a fucking baseball bat?"

He explained that he was in his room putting some clothes and other personal belongings in the duffle bag, and his mom barged in. She saw him packing and lost control.

"Where do you think you're going?" she asked him.
"I'm going to study."
"You're a liar! You can't even get your GED. You are a loser and will never amount to anything!"

She then barricaded the door, and they got into a pushing match, which resulted in Mark getting slapped across the face. After that, he figured it was game on, so he grabbed his bag and ran toward the door, dropping his shoulder like a fullback. He knocked her to the ground and continued to the front door. She instantly got up, grabbed the bat from his Little League days, and began the chase.

"Holy fuck! What a crazy fucking cunt!" I said in astonishment.

Then it hit me.

"Packing? Where are you going?" I asked, confused.
"That's the news I called you about. I knew my mom was listening on the other line, so I didn't want to say too much."

Earlier in the day, Mark was at Newsland, a retail store that sells newspapers from all over the world and magazines covering any topic you can think of—including the largest selection of pornographic magazines I had ever seen. I'm talking anything from *Playboy* to *Barely Legal* to weird fetish shit like midget lesbians to guys who like to pretend to fuck dead chicks—some real fucking sick shit.

Mark was browsing in the adult section when he started up a conversation with an old biker guy. They talked for a few minutes, and it turned out the guy wanted to purchase meth from Mark.

"Take a left here," Mark said, giving me directions.

They went to the guy's apartment and smoked meth for the rest of the day. Mark told the guy that he needed to move out of his parents' house but couldn't afford a place on his own. The guy struck up a deal: Mark could stay at his place as long as Mark got him high. Mark jumped on the proposal and went home to start packing.

We walked around the courtyard a couple times, looking for the correct building.

"There it is, building F." Mark pointed to the faded, barely visible letter on the side of the building.
"I have to warn you about a couple things," Mark said.
"Okay…"
"The first thing is that his name is Crazy."
"Crazy?" I repeated.

"Yeah."

"Really?"

"Yeah."

"Great, some tweaker who wants to be called Crazy. This should be fun. What else do I need to know?"

We walked into the hallway and approached the door. Mark knocked twice.

"He is also in a wheelchair and has some sort of speech impediment. I think he has MS or some shit."

The door opened.

"Hhhh……..iiiiiiiii   IIIIIII……..mmmmmmmm Crrrrraaaa……….zzzyyyyy," said the old, decrepit man in a wheelchair.

Thursday, September 26th

I spent the next few hours sitting on a couch listening to Crazy and Mark attempt to make small talk and smoke meth. That was the most I have ever smoked in one sitting; it was a constant flow of foilies being created, smoked, then crumpled up and thrown into a kitchen corner. I stopped counting when there were eight of them piled up against the wall.

Crazy was a small guy, weighing about 115 pounds, and if he wasn't in a wheelchair, he would only be about five feet six. His legs were deformed and had withered to almost nothing from years and years of being restricted to the wheelchair. If I had to guess, I would have said he was somewhere in his fifties or even early sixties.

"I have to take a piss," Mark blurted out as he made his way to the bathroom.

That left Crazy and me alone for the first time, sitting in awkward silence because I had no idea what to say. I was about to get up and grab a beer to break the tension when he slowly looked over at me and finally spoke.

"Y..ooo….uuuuu   aa…..rrrr……eeeeee ppprrroooo…..bbbb…aaaabbbb….lllllyyyyy woooo…..nnnnnndddddd….eeeeeerrrrr….iiiinnnnnngggg."

He struggled to speak and had to stop to take a breath after every few words. I waited.

"Www…hhhhyyyyyy   IIIII…….mmmm   iiiinnnnnn iiiii…..nnnnn   aaaaa   cccc…ccccchhhhhaaaiiirrrr."

I will translate: *"You are probably wondering why I'm in the chair."*

I never thought he was going to finish the simple sentence and wanted to give him a standing ovation for finally doing so.

"No, not at all! I'm just hanging out and getting high, man!" For some reason, I yelled it like he was deaf as well.

My answer did not sway him from telling his story. It began fifteen years earlier when he was a leader of a local biker gang. He pointed to the biker patches that were sewn onto his leather jacket.

He coordinated drug deals in a five-state radius. At the peak of the operation, his gang was delivering pounds of cocaine every week, and he was making tens of thousands of dollars every month.

One night he was out with his girlfriend, and they were celebrating their anniversary. After a few hours of drinking, he got down on one knee, took an engagement ring out of his pocket, and proposed to her. She said yes and they commenced a celebration.

It took him twenty minutes to get to this point in the story. Mark had returned and started preparing the next foily.

Crazy and his fiancé left at closing time and got on his motorcycle for the drive home. He sped in and out of traffic, reaching speeds of 120 mph. As he approached a bend in the road, he decided to pass a slow-moving car in front of him. Crazy accelerated past the car but did not see a semitruck approaching around the blind curve.

He swerved at the last moment but was too late. The truck collided with his bike, and they were thrown hundreds of feet into the air and landed on the embankment of the road.

He attempted to stand up to locate his girlfriend, but when he did, he couldn't feel his legs; they were lifeless and limp. He started yelling out her name but got no response. The only sound he could hear was the horn of the semitruck and an ambulance in the distance.

He began crawling in the direction where he thought she landed, and after many agonizing minutes, he finally reached her. She was barely hanging onto life; he attempted to revive her, but she died moments later in his arms. He held onto her until the paramedics had to pry him away from her.

It was a great, entertaining story—something out of a movie—but I didn't believe one fucking word of it. I would bet anything he had some sort of medical problem, and he fabricated the motorcycle crash story to make him look cool. I figured he was lonely and would do anything for company, including inventing some elaborate story and smoking meth all night long with two teenagers forty years younger than him.

I didn't care, though; that was more information than I wanted to know. I didn't want to know what really happened or how old he was or what his real name was; the less I knew about him, the better. He had money and a place to get high, and that was all that mattered to me.

Tuesday, October 1st

I woke up at 9:21 a.m. after sleeping for almost two days straight. Going to the bathroom and drinking a few glasses of water was the extent of my conscious activity for forty-eight hours. I felt like I could have slept another forty-eight.

After meeting Crazy, we went on a three-day meth bender. We locked ourselves in the apartment and smoked meth nonstop. We shut the blinds and covered the windows and screen door with blankets as an extra security measure to stop sunlight from making its way into the apartment.

We left the apartment only four times: once to purchase two rolls of tinfoil at 4:00 a.m., and the other occasions were to drive to Wheatridge to visit Mark's dealer.

We began with a teener and finished that by Thursday afternoon. Once the initial meth supply was depleted, Crazy rolled into his bedroom, returned with four twenties in his hand, and told us to go get more. We repeated that routine two more times when our meth supply reached empty. He was like a personal ATM on wheels.

I ran the calculations and came to the conclusion that I had been up for eighty-one hours straight. That was a personal record, but I was unsure if that was something I should be proud of.

My eyes were still adjusting to the sunlight shining into my room, but I could faintly see a yellow envelope on my nightstand. I rubbed my eyes a couple more times, attempting to focus, then sat up.

I opened the envelope, pulled out a card, and instantly looked at my calendar hanging on the wall. It was a birthday card from my parents. I had been so high I forgot my own fucking birthday.

Happy Birthday Scott!!! You are an amazing son, and we love you very much! Hopefully, you feel better so we can go out to dinner tonight. Love Mom and Dad!

A fifty-dollar bill was inside the card, and my thoughts immediately went to how much meth I could purchase with my birthday money.

"Fuck, I'm a piece of shit."

....

I was born twenty years earlier at Foundation Hospital in Portland, Oregon. I weighed 8.6 pounds and was twenty inches long. The summer before my senior year I was six feet tall and maxed out at around 215 pounds. I had more or less stayed that same weight since graduation.

The second night of our bender I weighed myself, and I was 187 pounds, down twenty-eight pounds in a few short months. The last time I weighed under 190 I was in the eighth grade. My cheekbones were becoming more and more visible, and my face was starting to look like I could have modeled for an anti-meth poster. I guess that was the result of doing meth almost every day for three months.

"They say it's your birthday. It's my motherfucking birthday too, you cocksuckers!" I sung as I waved the fifty-dollar bill in the air.

Monday, October 7th

My dad gave me an ultimatum: I had to find a job or he was going to kick me out of the house—and he seemed serious about it. Craig moving in didn't help the situation. We drove to a newspaper stand to get a *Denver Post*, and started searching the "Help Wanted" classifieds for any job that would be suitable for us and our drug routine.

By the time we were done, the paper resembled a streetlight with highlighter marks all over every page: circles, crosses, question marks with "maybe" or "call back later" or "fuck no" written in red, yellow, and green.

After a few hours, I started to become frustrated with the entire situation. Either the pay sucked, the hours sucked, the position sucked, or there was some combination of two of them—a few special jobs went three for three.

~~Pizza Hut Delivery Driver~~
~~Server~~
~~Valet Driver~~
~~Dishwasher~~
~~UPS Package Sorter~~
~~McDonalds Line Cook~~
~~7-Eleven Clerk~~
~~Telemarketer~~

I was about to give up and spend the afternoon drinking vodka when an ad caught my attention.

> *Local Movers Needed – Interview Today – Start Tomorrow*
> *Starting pay $9 an hour, weekends off and health insurance!*

That seemed like the perfect opportunity, better pay and better hours. I circled it with the green highlighter and threw the paper at Craig.

"Hey, check this out."

He looked at it and started nodding. "Let's go check it out," he said as he snorted a line.

We spent the next twenty minutes getting interview ready; button up shirt with my only pair of dress pants and shoes.

We found an empty parking lot a couple blocks from the moving company. Craig took a foily out of the glove box, took a hit, then passed it to me. I was getting to the point to where I required meth to help combat my anxiety.

"Dude, do you just want to come back tomorrow?" Craig asked.

He was trying to skip out on the interview, and I knew if we drove away now, we would never come back.

"We're here. We might as well see what they say," I responded. "Fine. Fuck it, let's go."

I decided it wouldn't look good if we walked into a job interview together, so I told Craig to wait five minutes. I wasn't sure what my theory was behind it; most likely it was the meth talking.

I went into the building, and the receptionist instructed me to sit in the lobby until the interviewer called my name. There were about ten other candidates in the lobby with me, and from the look of it, English wasn't their first language. If I had to guess, I would say they were Russian. This and the fact that I looked half the age of most of them boosted my confidence.

Craig entered the lobby less than two minutes later and sat on the opposite side of the room.

One after one, the Russians were called into the office. The lobby dwindled down to Craig, myself, and one other applicant who came in after us. Finally, a middle-aged, human resources lady called my name.

"Scott?"

I stood up and walked toward her with my hand extended and almost tripped in the process. After I regained my balance, I properly introduced myself and followed her into an office.

She asked the normal, textbook interview questions.

"Where do you want to be in five years?"

I thought about answering honestly: *I would literally shoot myself if I was at this fucking shit job in five years!* Or I could lie and say, *I would like to grow with the company and move into a management position.* Lying seemed the best option.

After about ten minutes, she offered me the position on the spot and asked if I could start the next day. I didn't want to, but I eagerly told her I would be there at 9:00 a.m. As I got up to thank her, she handed me a packet of papers.

"I almost forgot. Here's the paperwork for your drug test," she said.
"What was that?" I responded like I misheard her.
"Your drug test. It's a few blocks away, so stop there now or before work tomorrow."
"Oh yeah, of course."

I wanted to crumple the paper and throw it squarely in her face. I exited the office and just shook my head as I passed Craig in the lobby, knowing he was destined for the same drug-testing fate.

About twenty minutes later, Craig got into my truck and threw the packet on my dashboard in disgust.

"What the fuck are we going to do?" I asked.
Without hesitation, he said, "Sure-Jell and niacin."

I had known the answer, but I was hoping he would have a different solution. No such fucking luck.

My brother used Sure-Jell for drug tests in the Army and told me that everyone passed UAs after drinking it. Sure-Jell is a fruit pectin used to make jams and jellies and can be found at any grocery store for a few dollars. Just dump the powder into a two-quart pitcher, add water, mix, and drink the semisolid liquid. Imagine drinking Kool-Aid with large, undissolved chunks that almost induces vomiting after every swallow.

The next step was to take niacin. The medical purpose of niacin is to help lower cholesterol, reduce cardiovascular disease, and help other cardiovascular problems. A side effect is that it will flush the body.

The plan was to take twenty-five niacin to induce the flushing side effect while drinking the two quarts of Sure-Jell. That was our 100% guaranteed way to pass the drug test.

I spent the remainder of the evening wearing my boxers curled up in a ball on the floor in front of the air conditioner, burning up, turning bright red, and scratching almost every part of my body.

Friday, October 25th

We passed our drug tests and started that day. Our job consisted of unloading trucks that contained couches, bedroom sets, moving boxes, and countless other household items. We would then put everything into a numbered lot in the warehouse and wait until a different truck arrived to load the stuff we just unloaded into that truck so that truck could take the contents to the final moving location. The process seemed rather ludicrous and redundant to me, but they were paying me to do it, so I didn't ask questions.

The first three days we were model employees: showed up on time, worked late, did everything our foreman asked of us, and even worked every shift without getting high. We still got high, but we waited for the drive home.

On the fourth day, we took a few hits before work. By day eight we were on a regular smoke pattern, but instead of cigarettes we were smoking meth on every break.

This was our first payday, and all I wanted to do was grab my check, cash it, buy a baggie of crystal, and spend the weekend getting high. Unfortunately, I had to work my scheduled eight hours of monotonous loading and unloading first.

Craig returned from lunch a few minutes late and whispered in my ear. "I just got off the phone with Steve. He told me we could stop by his place after work."
"Serious?"
"Yeah! Now let's get to work so we can get the fuck out of here!"

....

Steve was in his thirties, married with two kids, and lived in an average split-level house in southwest Denver, and he was also a full-time meth salesman.

Up to this point, I had been buying meth from three types of so-called "meth dealers":

1. The dealer who bought in low quantities so that he could get high and make enough money to purchase his next product. This guy hoped to afford his habit by turning into a small-time dealer.
2. The dealer that said he could get you anything you required, but after sitting and listening to him make endless phone calls for hours, you knew there was a 50/50 chance of his fulfilling his promise.
3. The dealer who required the money up front before you received any product. Then you would have to sit and wait with your fingers crossed, hoping he would return.

Steve was an actual dealer, not a nickel and dimer. There were pros and cons into dealing with a guy like Steve. The pros were that I could purchase almost any amount of high-quality crystal meth, at any time of the day, as long as I had money. The cons were that there was a high level of danger. He dealt with a high volume of meth that involved a large amount of money, and he worked with paranoid guys who carried guns.

It was a risk I was willing to take.

Justin introduced Craig to Steve last summer, and he became their dealer, but since the Denny's episode happened with Justin, Craig had kept his distance.

Because of our recent struggles with finding a moral and reputable drug dealer, Craig called Steve. I think Craig held out contacting Steve because it vaulted us from the casual user to full-time crystal meth addict. It was scary to admit, but I felt we passed that point months ago. I had been pressuring Craig to introduce me to Steve since August. He finally gave in.

....

We arrived at Steve's house around 7:00 p.m. and parked directly in front of his house. I expected to see the house in disarray, with cars parked in the front yard and tweakers hanging out on the porch. To my surprise, the exterior of the house looked exactly like every other house on the block. The neighbors probably had no idea that inside the residence were pounds upon pounds of meth being exchanged on a regular basis.

Craig hesitated before pushing the doorbell.

"Try to keep your mouth shut."

In the time I had known Craig, I had never seen him look that serious. He wasn't fucking around.

Craig pushed the doorbell, and we waited in silence for an answer. I heard movement then the unlocking of the deadbolt. The door opened, and Craig walked in. I followed a few steps behind. I was now starting to get uneasy.

"Holy fuck, stranger! How you been?" Steve said as he wrapped his arms around Craig to give him a hug.

Steve was the definition of a meth dealer. He was at least six feet four and probably weighed less than 160 pounds. He had long brown hair that reached halfway down his back, but he was starting to bald on top. He wore skin-tight blue jeans with cowboy boots but didn't have a shirt on, even though it was late fall in Colorado.

He lived in a house and had no real job, but he had a keychain with about thirty keys on it—something that would make any apartment-complex maintenance man envious. The pièce de résistance of his attire was the Smith and Wesson 9 mm handgun attached to a holster on his hip.

Craig once told me a story about Steve that sounded more like an urban legend than real life. Steve was in the midst of a twenty-three-day meth bender without sleep. Yes, twenty-three days. I know it sounds like complete bullshit, but if you had seen this guy, you would believe it.

His diet during the bender consisted of crystal meth, Marlboro Reds, Mountain Dew, and Reese's Peanut Butter Cups. On the eve of his twenty-fourth night, he came to the realization that he was out of Mountain Dew, and he required it to function properly.

He devised a plan that had him driving 5 mph under the speed limit to the Total that was less than a mile from his house. He drew it out on a napkin, highlighting the one minor turn and two stop signs along the way. After preparing forty-five minutes for his journey, he was ready to go. He visualized himself driving to Total, purchasing two twelve-packs of Mountain Dew, and safely returning home.

The only problem was that it was all in his head. In reality, he was driving his tiny 1990 Honda CRX in excess of 75 mph down a residential side street that had a posted speed limit of 25 mph. He jumped a curb and hit a parked Chevy Suburban on the passenger's side, and both vehicles flew over fifty feet through the air until they landed in a field. The front end of the CRX completely disintegrated upon impact.

Steve crawled out of the mangled car and somehow managed to walk home without detection. When he arrived home, he was soaked in blood head to foot. His face, forehead, and neck were mangled.

As I stood in the hallway waiting for Steve to greet me, I looked for any visible scars, but I couldn't find any.

Steve finally looked past Craig and noticed me standing in the doorway.

"Who is this fucking guy?!" he asked as he placed his hand on the gun.

Saturday, October 26th

Crystal methamphetamine can be placed in a spoon and mixed with water until the solution is completely dissolved. Then use a cotton ball as a filter and pull back on the plunger of the syringe. The meth and water mixture will enter the barrel of the syringe. Select an arm, tie it off and inject the mixture into your veins.

Craig and I spent the entire night getting high with Steve. He told us stories about his experience of being up for twenty-three days, the car crash, completing enormous drug deals, and how he dismantled his pool table in the living room.

"I fucking saw these little blue people running across the table, and they were living in the pockets. In the fucking pockets! They resembled Smurfs, but Smurfs with long hair who were addicted to meth and trying to steal my supply. Those scandalous little fuckers!" Steve said.

I couldn't tell if he was joking or if he actually believed his stories; either way, he was one of the most charming and entertaining drug dealers I had ever met.

By 7:00 a.m., we had finished our original meth purchase and had to re-up. We bought another gram and decided it was time to leave. I did not want to leave, but I knew if we stayed at Steve's, we would be in a vicious cycle of storytelling, doing drugs, buying more drugs, then repeat. I knew we could easily lose track of the days and money if we remained in his drug dungeon.

We drove the short distance to Crazy's apartment. Both Steve and Crazy lived in the same white, middle-class neighborhood as Mark's parents. It was popular with Denver police officers because Denver County required all officers to live within the county, and this was as far south as you could go while still living in the county. It seemed like there was a Denver police car parked every ten houses or so.

When we arrived at Crazy's, Crazy, Mark, and Tony were doing meth as well and were wide awake from the previous night. We all seemed to be on the same level of highness, and I knew that was going to be trouble for the next few days.

Tony began shuffling a deck of cards and started explaining Spades; a card game he learned in one of his stints in jail. The four of us played cards, smoked meth, and drank for the next few hours.

"Dude, can you take me to Safeway for some cigarettes?" Craig asked me after we finished a hand.

I desperately needed to get out of that fucking apartment and get some fresh air, so I agreed. We made the short drive to Safeway and walked into the store.

"Follow me," Craig whispered.

I knew he was scheming something, so I followed him closely. He quickly weaved his way down aisles and past end displays. He picked up speed when his target was in sight.

"Where the fuck are you going?!" I said as I grabbed at his jacket.

I attempted to stop him, but he didn't acknowledge me. I pulled harder, but that just made him walk faster. Before I knew it, we were standing at the pharmacy counter.

A woman wearing a white smock with a name tag that read "Alice" approached us.

"How can I help you guys today?" she asked while scrutinizing us. "Hello, Alice. I'm a diabetic and just ran out of syringes. Is it possible to pick up replacements?"

She just stared at us—at Craig, then me, and then back to Craig. I was unsure if she was going to believe his bullshit story or if she was pressing the security button under the counter.

"Do you need a ten or twenty package?" Alice politely asked.

"Hmm. I guess I should just do twenty to be on the safe side."

Craig grabbed the syringes then jogged back to the front of the store to the first open register he could find. He was so excited he forgot the cigarettes.

Shooting, injecting, or slamming crystal meth results in the highest possible high, but it's the quickest way to create a dependency on it. Craig told stories about Justin shooting up and how quickly he changed. His enjoyment of getting high quickly transformed into a complete necessity, and the periods of happiness were few and far between.

Craig stood over Mark while Mark was pulling an orange extension cord around his lower bicep and continually making a fist to expedite the process of exposing his veins. Craig then flicked the syringe to remove any remaining air and hovered the tip of the needle over a vein that was bulging out of Mark's inner elbow. He slowly inserted the tip into a vein then pulled back on the plunger until a small amount of blood was visible in the chamber. He gradually pushed down on the plunger to ease the meth into Mark's bloodstream.

I started humming the melody of "Under the Bridge" by the Red Hot Chili Peppers.

Monday, October 28th

The five of us spent Sunday watching football and injecting crystal. The Broncos destroyed the Chiefs 34 to 7 with John Elway throwing three touchdowns. The Broncos were 7-1, and for me that was enough of a reason to celebrate.

We continued shooting and drinking all night long. Around 4:00 a.m., we ran out of meth, so everyone dispersed into different areas of the apartment. Craig lay on the couch in an attempt to rest before we had to work. Mark was in front of the fireplace with his CD player and headphones on. Crazy rolled into his room to do who knew what. Tony went into the bathroom around midnight and started throwing up. He had an allergic reaction from the crystal.

I remained at the kitchen table with the abundant amount of drug paraphernalia on the table and counter. The kitchen resembled a makeshift emergency room: needles, disposable gloves, and droplets of blood.

Out of the package of twenty, there were only four remaining needles that we hadn't used. Sixteen syringes among five guys in less than thirty-six hours; it was practically a blur. I couldn't even remember how many times I shot up.

The sight was disturbing. I grabbed a washcloth and a can of Lysol and began disinfecting the entire kitchen.

While I was cleaning, I spotted a needle hidden underneath an empty Bud Light can on the floor. It seemed like there was still crystal remaining in it, but I was unsure if I was hallucinating. I knelt down to examine it closer; it was real. I swiftly grabbed the needle and walked back into the kitchen. I then slithered behind the cabinets and onto the linoleum.

I wanted to use the needle but was worried about the possibilities of sharing a needle with those fucking drug addicts. One thing I actually learned in alcohol class was the dangers of sharing needles—AIDS, hepatitis and whatever other diseases you can get. I wouldn't have been surprised if one of them had some STD or some other blood-borne disease.

I did the calculations and started convincing myself that the odds were in my favor. There were five of us shooting up, so there was a twenty percent chance this was my needle. If that was the case, I wouldn't even be sharing. Then I came up with a scenario that the needle was never even used; it got knocked off the table and became lost. After a few minutes I decided that was the outcome of this particular needle. I deemed it was safe to use.

I took a peek into the living room to make sure Craig and Mark hadn't gotten suspicious about my recent activity. They were in the same position as the last time I looked.

I prepared my arm then slid the tip of the needle into my vein, pulled back, and then injected the remaining crystal meth into my body.

At that moment I realized I had just turned into the meth addict I always promised myself I would never become. I ignored the hazards of needle sharing to satisfy my own addiction. I wanted to cry, but I was incapable of producing tears.

I removed the needle and threw it to the other side of the kitchen, then put my head between my knees. I remained there for the next two hours until it was time to leave for work.

"Hey, we have to go, or we're going to be late," I said as I nudged Craig to get up.

I walked into the bathroom to brush my teeth, and Tony was still lying on the floor with chunks of vomit surrounding him. He didn't acknowledge that I entered the room, and at first I thought he might be dead. He finally grunted, though, and rolled over to escape the fluorescent bathroom light. As I was brushing my teeth, I noticed a bruise was forming on my inner elbow where I was shooting up. It was going to be a long-sleeved T-shirt day.

We arrived at work, clocked in, and started walking to our loading dock when we heard a voice over the intercom.

"Craig, please come to the office," a voice said out of the speakers.
"What the fuck is that about?" I asked with paranoia.
"I have no fucking idea. It can't be good."

I figured they knew we were high and were going to fire us. I sat on a moving box and waited for Craig to return with our final paychecks.

He finally appeared and tossed a pair of truck keys at me. I caught them, confused, and wondered what had occurred in the office.

"What the hell are these for"? I asked.
"They asked if I had a CDL, and I told them no. Then I said you do," he said with a smile.
"Are you fucking serious?"
"Yes, now let's go!"

We walked out to the truck terminal and located the moving truck we were supposed to be driving for our deliveries. It was fucking enormous at over thirty feet long.

I opened the door and sat in the driver's seat. There I was, strung out as fuck on zero sleep sitting behind the wheel of a 26,000-pound moving truck with ten gears, air brakes, and which required a Class B CDL. Driving this truck around Denver completely sober during morning rush hour traffic would be difficult, but driving high was the definition of insanity.

I turned the ignition on, placed my hand on the stick shift and stepped on the clutch.

"Fuck it, let's roll," I said.

Thursday, October 31st

Claire and I arrived at Crazy's apartment to find a room full of people: Mark, Jake, Craig, Tony, Samantha, Crazy, and a few others I didn't know or who aren't worth mentioning. Fifteen people crammed into 650 square feet with a bunch of booze, and a few quarters of meth almost always leads to trouble.

After a couple lines and a few beers, my worries diminished and I was ready to party. It was Halloween, and I wanted to get fucked up. The only problem was that I promised Claire I would get her home by 11 p.m. I kept dropping her off at home after her curfew, and her dad was getting pissed and threatened to ground her. He told her that if she was a minute late one more time he was going to put her under house arrest until the spring.

I didn't want to pick her up because I was going to have to drive her home at some point, and that meant I would have to stay somewhat sober. (Well, alcohol sober, not meth sober. I felt I could drive near perfection on any amount of meth.) I came up with every excuse I could think of not to pick her up, but she was not buying any of them.

"You'd rather get high and drunk with your friends than see me," she said.

She was right, but I couldn't tell her that.

"Fine, I will pick you up at six thirty. You fucking better be ready when I get there."

My plan was simple enough. Pick up Claire and get to the party by seven. Hang out, have a few drinks, do some crystal, then drive her home at ten-thirty and be back to party by eleven thirty. That would give me the rest of the night to get fucked up.

We spent the next few hours drinking, snorting, smoking, and being loud then yelling louder in an attempt to get everyone to be quiet. Sometimes it worked, sometimes it didn't, but eventually it was to no avail. The more substances we consumed, the louder the volume on the CD player went, which in turn made everyone talk louder and which would eventually make the CD player be turned up to overtake the talking.

Claire and I snuck out to my truck so we could have sex. Fucking in the cab of the truck is tough; space is confined with no extra room to stretch out or move. I just sat on the passenger side and made her do all the work; I was completely fine with that.

An elderly man stopped almost directly in front of my truck so his dog could take a piss, and he looked directly inside my truck. I'm sure the visual of Claire bouncing up and down was hard to comprehend at first and then quite the spectacle. I waved, and he turned away in disgust.

We completed, freshened up, then returned to the party. I was keeping a tally of the beers I drank on my palm. There were five marks written in a black marker staring back at me, and it was only nine fifteen. I was ready to take Claire home.

"Hey, are you about ready?" I asked.

She looked at her watch then glared at me.

"Are you serious? I don't have to be home for two hours, and it only takes thirty minutes to get there," she said.
"Well, I just—"
"I'm sick of your fucking excuses. You just want to take me home, so you can get fucked up!"
"Fine, we can wait!"

I walked into the kitchen, got a Bud Light, grabbed a pen, punctured the side of the can, and shotgunned the beer within a few seconds. I was to the point where I didn't care about my consequences; I was going to drink and drive her home. If I made it back—great. If I got a DUI, I'd worry about that when I sobered up.

We spent the rest of the night about as far apart as two people could be inside a tiny apartment. Finally, around ten fifteen she walked up to me.

"Can we go?" she asked.
"Yeah."

I went to the bathroom to cleanse my mouth with Scope and splashed water on my face in some attempt to sober up. After staring at myself in the mirror, I walked into the kitchen, grabbed my keys, then walked out the front door without saying a word to anyone.

She sensed I was pissed, and we barely spoke on the drive from Littleton to Wheatridge. I turned the stereo volume as loud as it could go; the decibels were probably close to the level that caused ear damage. Even if she tried to yell, she wouldn't be able to overcome the music.

When I arrived at Claire's house, she leaned in to kiss me.

"I love you so much, and I'm sorry for starting a fight."
"I'm sorry. I love you too, babe," I softly said.

We made out for a few minutes until she got out of my truck and walked up the driveway.

That was a lie. I was sure as fuck not sorry and not even sure if I loved her, but I knew if I responded in any other way, it would have created an argument that would have delayed my arrival back at the party. Sometimes it's better just to shut the fuck up and smile.

I drove 20 mph over the posted speed limit down the ten-mile stretch of Wadsworth Boulevard, one of Denver's north-south arterial roads. I made it back to Crazy's in record time.

When I arrived back at the apartment, the place was almost empty. Crazy was in his bedroom, a few people were passed out in the living room, and some girl was in the kitchen on the phone. She almost looked like she could be Claire's little sister.

"Are you Scott?" she asked.

I nodded, and she handed me a note from Mark.

Yo dude, we went to some chicks house in Boulder. Page me and I'll give you directions.

"Those fucking assholes!"

Boulder is about thirty minutes north of Claire's house, so there was no way I was going to drive another hour back up north for some house party that could have been a complete bust. I crumpled up the piece of paper and threw it across the living room.

I shoved a passed-out guy off the couch and onto the floor and then sat down. While I was cutting a line, I overheard the girl on the phone; she was looking for a ride home.

"Why didn't you go to the party?" I asked her.
"Mark asked if I wanted to go, but I have to be home by midnight, so I couldn't."
"Well, it's almost midnight," I said, pointing to the wall clock.
"I know. My friend was on her way, but she bailed on me so now I'm totally screwed."
"That sounds like a pickle," I responded in a sarcastic tone. She was not amused and started dialing another number.

I got off the couch and walked to the kitchen table.

"Hey, I'm Scott."
"Hi, I'm Kelsey."

I started talking to her and found out she lived only a couple blocks from my parents. I figured I had two options at this point:

1. Sit and wait, hoping everyone would return. The best-case scenario would have been two hours at the earliest.
2. Drive Kelsey home and try to fuck her.

I decided on option two. I offered her a ride home and within minutes we were driving on Belleview to her parents' house. At the first stop light, I made a move to kiss her and she didn't resist. It was almost too easy.

We held hands the rest of the drive, and she guided me to her house. I parked a few houses away so her dad wouldn't see my truck dropping her off. We started making out, then I moved my hand up under her shirt. After what I deemed was a good amount of foreplay, I made the move to unbutton her pants.

"I'm sorry. I can't do this," she said as she backed away from me.
"Is everything okay?" I asked in a concerned tone.
"Well, I really want to hang out with you again, but I can't sleep with you because I just met you."
"That's totally fine! I wasn't trying to have sex with you. I'm sorry if that's what it seemed like."

Tuesday, November 5th

> *You see, I think drugs have done some good things for us, I really do. And if you don't believe drugs have done good things for us, do me a favor; go home tonight, take all your albums, all your tapes, and all your CDs and burn 'em.' Cause you know what, the musicians that made all that great music that's enhanced your lives throughout the years... real fucking high on drugs. —Bill Hicks*

When you're high, it feels like most songs were written about drugs. There's a word, phrase, or line that connects the song to the addict. They envision the song is about snorting cocaine, tripping on acid, or injecting heroin.

The largest rock bands in the world wrote songs about drugs: "Mr Brownstone" (heroin) by Guns N' Roses, "Lucy in the Sky with Diamonds" (LSD/acid) by the Beatles, "Kickstart my Heart" (speedball—a cocaine/heroin mixture) by Motley Crue, and "Cocaine" (I guess this one is a little more obvious than the others.) by Eric Clapton.

Musicians we idolized are self-admitted druggies who get arrested, are constantly in and out of drug rehab, and in some cases, overdose and die. The musicians that did die from overdoses got propelled into legendary status. Jimi Hendrix, Jim Morrison, and Sid Vicious became larger the moment they overdosed and died— front-page headlines, cult-status stories, and even feature films. Fuck, even Elvis died of a mixture of codeine, morphine, valium, Quaaludes, Demerol, and ten other prescription drugs.

Concerts are enhanced with alcohol and drug usage. When you are under the influence, you can feel each hit of the snare drum, strum on the guitar, and each high note of the vocalist. It is a euphoric high that I have not experienced on any other level, and I am not sure anything can compare to it.

I think that is why music has such a connection to addicts. It can feel like the band is playing directly to you and what you are experiencing in your life. Music makes you smile, makes you cry, makes you remember a place in time, can touch your soul, and make life a lot more livable.

....

This was the start of three concerts in nine days: Tool at the Mammoth Event Center, Deftones on Saturday the 9th at the Ogden Theatre and Stone Temple Pilots on Thursday the 14th at McNichols Sports Arena.

I spent two days sleeping, eating, and resting my body to prepare for this nine-day expedition of music, drugs, and alcohol. Craig and Mark were on a mission to get higher than we had ever been. They put together a meth fund and raised $650, with Craig throwing in almost a third of that. Craig returned from Steve's with fourteen grams of crystal meth, almost a half-ounce, enough meth to supply a small army of junkies … or the five of us.

Craig poured the entire contents of the baggie onto the kitchen table and formed a yellow/white powder mountain that was inches high. It was our *Scarface* moment. I had never seen that much crystal at one time, and it was exciting and intimidating at the same time.

The federal prison sentence for possession of five to forty-nine grams of pure meth is a minimum of five years for the first offense. Depending on how much our product was cut with, we had enough in our possession that would put us all in prison for at least half a decade.

I was concerned that I would not be able to handle a nine-day drug binge and considered skipping the first show. I brainstormed different excuses I could use to skip it, but knew I would get peer-pressured into going, so I just kept my mouth shut.

On a side note, it was also Election Day. By the time I woke up, the results were almost final. Bill Clinton defeated Bob Dole in a landslide to extend his term as the forty-second president. Clinton carried thirty-one states compared to Dole's nineteen.

This was the first presidential election I could have participated in, but I chose to sleep and prepare for my concert and drug marathon. I would have most likely voted for Clinton, but Bob Dole won Colorado, receiving the eight electoral votes, so my vote would have been for not.

I watched the news coverage and snorted a line to celebrate Mr. Clinton's reelection.

Thursday, November 14th

I looked down and saw Mark holding a foily in front of me.

"Are you going to fucking hit this?" he asked in an irritated tone.
"What?"
"I've asked you three fucking times if you wanted to hit this!"
" No, I'm good."

I was actually far from good; I was disoriented and confused. I was sitting in the driver's seat, my hands on the steering wheel, and all I could see was brake lights in front of me. I looked down at the clock displaying 5:20; we were sitting in rush hour traffic on northbound I-25.

I don't remember driving to that point, I don't remember walking to my truck. I suspected we were driving to McNichols Arena to see Stone Temple Pilots, but I was too embarrassed to ask. I pulled the ticket out of the ashtray; it confirmed my speculation.

I started thinking back over the previous few days, and everything was coming up empty. Wednesday was blank, Tuesday blank, Monday blank, Sunday blank as well. I barely recalled taking Claire home on Saturday night, but that was my most recent memory. I had a complete and total blackout for five fucking days—zero recollection if I had slept, ate, went to work, or robbed a bank. Well, I guess I would have some sort of idea if I robbed a bank, but you get the idea.

I turned on the right blinker and changed lanes.

"What the fuck are you doing?" Mark asked.
"I have to take a piss real quick."

That was a lie. I just needed to get out of my truck, and re-group. I turned off on the closest exit and drove to a convenience store a few blocks off the highway.

I walked into the store, grabbed the key attached to a three-foot stick, and made my way to the bathroom. I examined myself in the mirror. I was white as a ghost, and it looked like I had just thrown up. I looked down at my shirt and pants to see if there was evidence of vomit, but I was clean. My pupils were exceedingly dilated, and I could barely see the blue in my eyes. My image in the mirror was blurry, and I couldn't focus on any part of my face.

I turned the faucet on full blast and held my hands under the hot water until I could no longer bear it. Once it got to that point, I started splashing water onto my face. It felt like I was burning my skin, but I needed to do something to help snap me out of my drug-induced amnesia. I continued to splash water with my left hand and started slapping myself as hard as I could with my right.

Knock! Knock!

I instantly froze.

"What you doing in there? Bathroom for customers only!" I heard in broken English from the other side of the door.
"One second!" I yelled.

My face was bright red, and my shirt was drenched. I turned off the water and started pulling paper towels out of the dispenser in some attempt to clean myself up; it was a no-win situation.

"Fuck it" I said to myself.

I opened the door to an Asian guy standing in the hallway.

"Here you go," I said as I handed him the key.

He just stared at me. He was about to yell again but stopped when he saw my appearance.

I walked to the back of the store and grabbed a Coke out of the cooler. I dropped two dollars on the counter and walked to the entrance without my change or saying a word. I continued into the parking lot but quickly realized I was going in the wrong direction and had to turn around. I could see Mark laughing at me from inside my truck.

"Did you just piss yourself?" he asked. He was laughing harder.
"Just shut the fuck up and hold this!" I said as I handed him the Coke.

....

Stone Temple Pilots (STP) was one of the biggest rock bands in the world. They sold almost ten million records over the course of four years and three albums. The lead singer, Scott Weiland, publicly battled drug addiction practically from the start of the band's success.

He was arrested in May of 1995 in Pasadena, California, when sheriff's deputies found heroin in his wallet and cocaine in his vehicle. It was his third drug-related arrest in less than two years. He was spared jail time on the condition that he went to rehab and drug counseling.

He completed an inpatient program and moved into a halfway house in Pasadena in early 1996. STP released their third album, *Tiny Music... Songs from the Vatican Gift Shop* on March 26th, 1996, and scheduled a full US tour in support of the album.

Shortly after the release of that album, STP announced that Scott had relapsed and entered a drug-rehabilitation facility, thereby canceling the spring and summer tour dates. He spent the summer in a court-ordered program at the Impact Alcohol and Drug Treatment Center in Pasadena.

They returned to the stage on November 1st, 1996, at the Viper Room in Hollywood—ironically, the location of the heroin overdose and death of actor River Phoenix.

I began to wonder if a guy like Scott Weiland—who had millions of dollars and access to the leading drug counselors in the preeminent rehab facilities couldn't stay clean, what fucking chance did I have?

"Going blind, out of my damn reach; somewhere stuck in the fucking vaseline," I muttered.

Friday, November 15th

"Do you see that?" I asked Mark as I frantically blinked my eyes in an attempt to focus my vision.

"I am seeing a lot of weird shit right now!" he casually responded.

That was not the response I was looking for.

I was driving 75 mph on Interstate 70, the highway that connects Denver to the mountain towns and ski villages to the west. I was trying to comprehend what I saw out of the corner of my eye.

In the embankment to my right, it looked like a group of teenagers was about to make a run across the highway a few hundred feet in front of me. They were crouched on the side of the road waiting for the opportunity to make their move. It was fucking midnight in the middle of a cold November night. I knew there was no way this could be real.

I closed my eyes and shook my head, hoping the visual would vanish when I reopened my eyes. It didn't. I had to make a quick decision on the impending predicament. Slamming on my brakes would be my normal instinct, but there was nothing normal about this situation. Stopping in the middle of the highway at a high speed would result in an accident. If it was not a hallucination, and it was a group of drunken kids running across the highway, I would most likely hit and kill them.

I thought back to Steve telling us about seeing tiny blue people running across his pool table. At that moment, I thought he was a fucking lunatic; but I was now faced with a similar dilemma.

"Fuck it," I whispered.

I grasped the steering wheel and clinched it as hard as I could. I looked to my left so I would not be tempted to swerve if I saw them in the middle of the road. As I passed the mile marker where they were perched, I looked over to my right to see exactly what nearly caused a rear-end collision.

It was a tumbleweed stuck to a pole that was blowing in the wind.

"A fucking tumbleweed!"
"What?" Mark asked.
"Nothing."

I wanted to get out and burn that fucking weed to ashes, but I decided pulling over on a major highway to start a small brush fire would not be the smartest decision in my condition. I continued driving, focusing directly in front of me so I would not have any outside distractions.

As we made our way closer to Littleton, Mark asked me if I wanted to go to Crazy's with him. I declined. I could not handle any more drugs or alcohol. I dropped him off then drove home.

I sat on my bed and paged Kelsey with a 911 code. I was about to go upstairs to the bathroom when the phone started ringing.

"Are you okay?" she asked.
"I just don't feel very good."
"What's wrong?"
"Everything," I responded, laughing.
"Do you need anything?"
"It would be cool to hang out with you."
"I can sneak out and walk over … be there in twenty minutes. Does that work?"
"It's perfect."

....

I woke up in my bed with the alarm clock flashing 6:28. I looked down and saw someone in my bed; the top of her head was in my armpit so I could not see her face. I was assuming it was Kelsey, but after last night I would not be shocked if it was some other random girl.

I slowly removed my arm from underneath her head, and leaned up to get a better vantage point. It was Kelsey.

I lifted up the blankets to go take a piss and noticed that we were both naked. I started racking my brain for any memory of the previous night. I remembered her showing up at my house, and faintly remember making out. I remained perplexed, then I remembered an important detail, she told me that she was a virgin. I was unsure if that happened or if it was another hallucination.

I stood up and started searching for my boxers, but it wasn't an easy task because clothes were scattered all over the floor. I finally found them next to my dresser.

I walked upstairs to the bathroom and flipped on the light. I dropped my boxers and started to piss. My eyes were still adjusting to the light when I looked down and noticed that there was blood on my penis. I startled myself until I realized that it must be from Kelsey.

"My fucking luck! The first virgin I fuck, and I'm so strung out that I don't remember it."

I was sitting on the couch next to my uncle watching the Thanksgiving football game. The Chiefs beat the Lions 28 to 24. Barry Sanders was held to seventy-seven rushing yards.

"Good game."
"It was," I responded as we watched the post-game show.

The house was at full capacity. My parents were upstairs cooking the turkey, my brother along with his wife and kid were in the backyard, my grandma was taking a nap on the couch upstairs, and there were other family members scattered throughout the house.

The aromas of the turkey, mashed potatoes, and pumpkin pie were filling up the entire house, and I could not escape them. I wanted to puke at the thought of eating.

I had been doing meth almost every day for the last four weeks on a bodybuilder schedule: four days on meth and one day off to relax, recover, and sleep. I was in a constant state of being high and exhausted. Minutes, hours, and days all blended together; everything seemed like a dream. I had no idea it was Thanksgiving until I went upstairs and saw my mom preparing the turkey.

I could feel my body wasting away. My mouth hurt, my muscles ached, my bones ached, and my weight loss made me look like I had contracted AIDS.

Up to that point, I had avoided getting meth sores, or "meth mites," associated with meth addicts. The sores usually occur from constant picking at a problem area, and that becomes larger and larger and then usually spreads to other areas. The sores take longer to heal because meth restricts blood flow to the infected area. A few days before Thanksgiving I got my first meth sore, it was on my forearm. It was small compared to others I had seen, so I considered myself lucky.

My main concern was my teeth because they were in constant pain. Meth depletes the body of calcium, the vitamin essential to maintaining healthy teeth. It also includes acidic ingredients that can damage teeth. The ingredients include but are not limited to battery acid: Drano, over-the-counter cold medications like Sudafed, antifreeze, engine starter fluid, and brake fluid. Basically, pop the hood of your car and you can find the ingredients you need to cook meth. I'm no dentist, but I came to the conclusion that was the root of my tooth pain.

My diet primarily consisted of French fries and strawberry shakes, softer fast-food items that were easy to chew and swallow. Two days before Thanksgiving I was chewing a piece of Juicy Fruit, and my gums started bleeding. I had to spit it out because it hurt, and I was worried the gum might pull out a tooth. I had not eaten since.

I could hear my mom setting the table upstairs, so I knew dinner was getting close. I excused myself from the living room in an attempt to find a vacant area in the house to snort a quick line. My bedroom did not have a lock, and I was worried about someone accidently walking in and catching me mid-snort. That was too risky. My truck became an option, but I was worried about a nosey neighbor walking their dog. I even thought about walking out the front door and not coming back for a few days, but I knew my mom would disown me.

The bathroom seemed like the safest bet, even though it was a revolving door of family members. I could lock the door and that eased my nerves. I waited for the opportune moment to sneak in quietly when nobody was watching. I peeked into the kitchen and saw everyone captivated by the turkey and took this as my opportunity to access the bathroom.

I locked the door, turned on the fan, and started placing the essential equipment on the counter: meth, driver's license, and tooter. I carved out a three-inch line on the counter with ID and picked up the tooter.

Knock, Knock.

"Scott? Are you in there?" my mom asked.

I knew the moment I decided to get high that would happen. I wasn't sure if I should answer or snort the line first. I answered.

"Yeah?" I said, covering the line because I felt she had X-ray vision and could see directly through the door.
"I'm just letting you know we are about to start dinner."
"Ok. I will be up in a second."

I waited a solid ten-count to ensure she was not still standing in the hallway then snorted the line. I wiped down the counter with the hand towel to remove any excess residue.

When I arrived in the kitchen, everyone was properly sitting at the table waiting for me. I sat down next to my brother and tilted my head down to avoid making any kind of eye contact. Everyone at the table got quiet. I felt it was the start of an intervention.

"Scott, do you want to say grace?" my mom asked.

I could barely string together a couple words, and my mom wanted me to recite a prayer that I hadn't said in years. I gradually looked up at her.

"Sorry, I really don't remember it."
"I can help you with it," she responded.
"Please, you just do it," I harshly responded. She got the point.

I lowered my head again as she began to pray. After she finished, the food was passed in my direction. I wanted to throw every plate against the wall. I knew there was no conceivable way I could eat, and I was going to have to do my best to fake it.

My plan was to take a tiny piece of turkey then bury it with mashed potatoes and stuffing and drown the entire plate with gravy, kind of a Thanksgiving soup. This would give the illusion that I was eating without having to put anything solid down my throat.

I quietly smiled and politely listened to the conversation while I put a fork-ful of Thanksgiving dinner in my mouth, choking down every bite.

Saturday, November 30th

After I said goodbye to the last Thanksgiving straggler, I walked downstairs into my room and dropped a quarter of a gram into a bulb. I lit the flame and inhaled the smoke into my mouth. With each hit, I savored the flavor of the meth almost like a wine connoisseur tasting a fine glass of Merlot.

After finishing the bulb, I started searching my VHS movie collection. I picked out *Pulp Fiction* then slid the movie into my VCR, pressed play, and got comfortable on my bed, preparing to enjoy the movie.

Around the dance scene with Vincent Vega and Mia Wallace, I suddenly felt my heart skip a beat and came close to blacking out. It felt like my heart actually stopped beating for a few seconds. That was the worst experience I had on meth, and I was positive I was overdosing.

I feared that I might lose consciousness and pass out, so I instantly sat up and began to evaluate the situation:

1. Breathe. That one should be easy; I had been doing it my entire life.
2. Check my pulse. It was racing, and I could barely keep the tally.
3. Remain calm. Panic would only make things worse.
4. Locate the phone in case it happened again, so I could dial 911.

I wasn't sure if I was having a heart attack, if the constant meth usage was slowly destroying my heart and arteries, or if I was having a severe panic attack. Either way, the feeling scared the shit out of me.

I gathered my composure then dropped to my knees, placed my elbows on my mattress, intertwined my fingers, and began to pray.

I was raised Catholic but as I grew older, I stopped attending church and lost my faith completely around high school. I wasn't sure if praying would help, but it was the only thing I could think to do at that moment. I looked up to the white spackled ceiling.

"Hello God? I hope all is good up there. I know it's been a little while, but I'm scared. ... I'm really fucking scared. Sorry for cursing , but I don't want to die. I promise if you get me through this, I'll stop doing meth."

I paused.

"Okay, we both know that is a lie. How about two weeks?"

Pulp Fiction was still playing in the background. Mia Wallace just snorted the heroin.

"Okay! Let's say one week! One solid week of no meth, deal? Deal? Deal! Thanks, buddy."

I stood up and got lightheaded in the process, almost falling to the floor.

"Mental note: next time I think I might be overdosing, do not make any sudden movements."

I lowered myself onto the bed and rested my head on a pillow, attempting to enjoy the rest of the movie. I attached my left hand to my right wrist, constantly checking my pulse.

....

I received a call from Roger, a guy I went to high school with. His parents were out of town, and he was planning a house party. I told him I would stop by since it was only a few blocks from my parents'. I turned off the phone and tossed it onto the couch on the other side of my room. I stood up beside my bed, contemplating whether I should go and started having an internal conflict with myself.

"I need a break from meth and booze. I'm going to kill myself," I said as I sat down.
"It'll be fun, and there will probably be some fuckable girls there." I stood up.
"If I can't go a weekend without drugs, I have a real fucking problem." I sat down.
"Drink beer and stay away from any crystal. Have fun and don't be a fucking pussy."

I stood up, and grabbed my keys.

The moment I arrived at the party, I knew I had made a mistake. The party mostly consisted of people I despised from high school. I grabbed a Old Style and started searching for a familiar face.

I was walking down a hallway when I ran into Craig.

"Let's go," he said with his hand on my forearm.

Craig ushered me into a hallway bathroom and locked the door behind him. Mark and Roger were inside waiting for our arrival. The tiny hallway bathroom only had a toilet with a sink; we were practically standing on top of each other.

Mark was slicing up lines on a Dr. Dre *The Chronic* CD case while everyone watched in anticipation. Music and laughter could be heard from the other side of the door. I envied the people enjoying the party and did not want to be trapped in that fucking bathroom. I really did go to the party with every intention of staying away from meth; that plan lasted all of about twenty minutes. I knew if there was a God, I was going to face my consequences for breaking my promise.

Craig snorted his line then passed the CD case to me. I kindly offered it to Mark to allow him to do his line then offered it to

Roger for his. I knew going last meant I would receive the smallest line out of the four. Addicts want to do the maximum amount of drugs possible, so if one line looked one millimeter longer, that is the line that they would pick. Since I decided to do crystal, I wanted to keep it to a minimum.

Afterwards, we casually exited the bathroom and rejoined the rest of the party. After a few beers, Andre walked up to me.

"Hey, can we talk outside real quick?" he asked.
"Yeah, of course."

I followed him out onto the patio with no idea what he wanted to talk about. He lit up a Marlboro and started to speak.

"I've known you since middle school. Fuck, we even played little league together."
"Yeah, we go way back," I responded.
"Well, you're one of my good friends, and I love you man, but I am really worried about how much meth you've been doing lately," he said.

I was dumbstruck. I wanted to know how this hypocrite thought he could lecture me about my drug usage. He once took forty-five Dramamine pills, and ended up in the emergency room. He thought the clock on the wall was the cartoon pizza guy from the Little Caesars commercials.

"It seems like you've been going overboard lately, and you look like shit. Look at your fucking face."

I just nodded, but deep down I wanted to punch him square in his face and beat the living shit out of him.

"Sorry, I didn't want to make a big deal out of it. I just wanted to let you know I'm here to help."
"Thanks for the concern, pal," I said.

He offered a handshake, but I ignored it and walked back into the party.

That was the last time I saw Andre.

Saturday, December 7th

I was lying on the floor in Crazy's apartment in front of the fireplace trying to relax after a long night of partying. Craig and his fuck buddy of the week, Kara, were on the loveseat. Tony and Jake were on the couch. Mark was lying in the hallway; Crazy was in his room, and Claire was next to me.

It was 4:30 a.m. and everyone was either passed out or trying to get there. Claire fell asleep hours ago, and I could hear Tony and Jake snoring. Our community supply of crystal ran out Friday night, so we purchased a handle of McCormick vodka and finished it off in a few hours. Everyone was either drunk or running on meth fumes.

I had secretly removed a couple rocks from the baggie we purchased Friday afternoon and stashed them in my pocket. After we ran out of our community supply, I started going into the bathroom to snort lines solo. I felt filthy that I had come to these tactics, but I had a feeling Mark and Craig were doing the same. That was my justification.

There was no way I could sleep, but I couldn't give the impression I was high, so I just put on my headphones, placed the Alice in Chains *MTV Unplugged* CD into my Discman and pressed play. My goal was to close my eyes and drift into some sort of meth dream state.

The opening chords of "Nutshell" had started when I suddenly felt a hard kick on the sole of my Vans. I tilted my head to see who it was.

"Dude! You have to come in Crazy's room right now!" Mark said in a panic.

I immediately knew something was wrong. I pulled my headphones off and pushed the Discman from my chest.

"What's up?" I said as I sat up. I heard noise coming from the bedroom, but I could not pinpoint the sound.
"Crazy's going into convulsions or some shit! I have no idea what the fuck is going on! What the fuck are we supposed to do?"

I jumped off the floor and ran to the bedroom. When I arrived in the doorway, I got my first glimpse of Crazy. I was shocked. He was bouncing off the bed like Linda Blair in *The Exorcist*. His arms and legs were flailing in every direction while his torso was bouncing a few inches off the mattress. I was hypnotized watching him.

Mark finally hit me in the arm. "What the fuck are we going to do?"

I snapped back into reality.

"I don't know. Get him some water or some shit," I said as I walked past Mark on my way into the living room.

By this time, the commotion had woken everyone else up, and they made their way into the hallway.

I grabbed my backpack and started throwing any drug-related items I could find into it—tooters, tin foil, light bulbs, pipes, and empty baggies. I even put the silver serving tray that we used to cut lines on into my bag—well, after I licked it clean.

Claire, Jake, Craig and Kara all came back into the living room. Craig said something to me, but I was in a trance, so I did not respond. I continued filling my bag with any incriminating evidence.

Out of the corner of my eye, I saw Claire pick up the cordless phone and turn it on. I dropped everything I was holding and ran toward her. Her index finger dialed "9" on the keypad and I slapped the phone out her hand before she could press "1." The phone slammed against the floor with so much force the battery pack became dislodged.

"What the fuck are you doing?!" I yelled.
"I'm calling an ambulance!" Claire said in confusion.
"Bullshit! No fucking way! Not while I am here!"
"He's overdosing and going to die if we don't do anything!" She screamed at me.
"I don't fucking care! That's the fucking risk he signed up for by doing crystal!" I responded with no remorse.

She helplessly stared at me. I placed my hands on her shoulders and grabbed them as hard as I possibly could.

"If you want to call 911 and wait around until the paramedics and cops show up, be my fucking guest. Have fun explaining why you're hanging out with some sixty-year-old cripple who just fucking overdosed on meth. But you are going to wait until I am in my truck and out of this fucking apartment complex."

The room was completely silent. She began to cry.

"I'm leaving in thirty seconds! Whoever wants to come with me, grab your shit and get the fuck out of here!" I announced to the room.

Jake, Tony, Kara and Craig all grabbed their personal items and ran out of the apartment. Claire was standing in the living room motionless.

"Trust me, Claire, you don't want to be a part of this, Mark can handle it. He will think of something! Now let's go." I grabbed her arm and guided her to the front door.
"Mark!" I yelled as I made my final preparations before I left. The gurgling sounds from the bedroom were becoming louder.

He ran into the hallway.

"Dude, sorry, but we have to go. Good luck man!" I said.

He nodded and ran back into the bedroom. I put my backpack over my shoulder, and jogged to the parking lot.

Tuesday, December 10th

Craig was getting dressed for work inside Kara's house and I went outside to warm up my truck and scrape the frost off the window. It was a bitter cold morning, and my truck was still churning out cold air through the vents. I was not sure if I was shivering from the cold or the meth.

Craig strolled down the pathway and got into my truck. I drove away without either of us saying a word. I turned up the radio and focused my attention on the cars in front of me. About twenty minutes into our forty minute drive to work Craig pulled his pager out.

"It's Tim. Go to a payphone!" Craig said.

I formed a tiny smile. Tim was our manager, and I knew him paging us this early meant one of two things:

1. We were fired.
2. There was not enough work for us, so we got the day off.

Either way, I did not care.

I drove to the nearest 7-Eleven and parked next to the pay phone. Craig grabbed thirty-five cents out of the ashtray and ran to the phone. I watched him dial and attempted to read his body language waiting for any type of reaction, good or bad.

After a couple minutes, he finally gave me a thumbs-up! He hung up and skipped back to the truck.

"Let's go back to your place so I can shower and make a few phone calls."
"Sounds good!" I responded.

I exited the parking lot and proceeded to speed all the way home through morning traffic. The plan was to shower, get ready, and be in and out of my house in under an hour. My mom was home on vacation, so the less I had to converse with her the better.

We walked into the living room, and the house was ominously silent. I looked back outside, and my mom's Ford Explorer was parked in the driveway. I knew she was home. I proceeded with caution as I walked down the stairs to my room.

When I walked into my room, my mom was sitting on the edge of my bed, and I could tell she had been crying.

"What is this?" she asked in a barely audible tone.

She then moved her hand from behind her back and raised it directly in front of her face. She was holding an opened package that contained four or five syringes.

My head dropped.

I knew they were not mine. I had not shot up in weeks, and when I did, I always did it at Crazy's. I may have been a meth addict with poor judgment and morals, but I would never have been careless to leave unattended needles in my room.

I turned back to Craig, who was looking directly at the ground. He knew they were his. He had been crashing on my couch for a few straight weeks and was shooting up almost daily. I waited for him to admit they were his—for him to say something, anything—but he didn't. He was just a silent coward.

"What are these?" she asked with more authority.

I glared at Craig but quickly came to the conclusion he was not going to utter a word, so I said the only words that came to mind.

"They are not mine." I hopelessly said.

The response irritated her. She sprung up and threw the package at me. It bounced off my chest and landed between my feet. One of the needles fell out of the bag.

"Then where did they come from and how did they get into my house?!"

I could no longer look at her, so I just closed my eyes.

"They are not mine," I said, shaking my head.
"Tell me now or get out of my house!"
"They are not mine," I barely uttered. I could not conceive a lie that would be somewhat believable at that point.

It was a battle I was not going to win, so I turned to the door. Craig had already made his exit. I made it a couple steps then felt a tug from behind. My mom was pulling the handle on my backpack.

"Open your goddamn backpack!" she yelled. It was the loudest I had ever heard her voice.

I planned on fighting her to the death over the contents of the backpack.. The bag contained a half gram of meth, a box of tin foil, and most of the drug paraphernalia from the night Crazy had a seizure. It was like a meth treasure chest, and there was no way that I would ever let her look inside. I quickly turned away as she attempted to unzip the main compartment.

"No," I said.
"Give me your bag right now!" she said, sobbing.

I only shook my head back and forth. I could no longer speak.

"Give me that bag or get the fuck out of this house, Scott, and never come back!" She was full-blown crying now.

That was the first time I had ever heard my mom curse. I knew I was a disappointment to her; I was a fucking disappointment to myself. It took the highest level of self-control not to start crying. I just wanted to tell her that I was a drug addict, and I did not know what to do, and I was scared about what was going to happen to me. I just wanted to hug her and have her tell me that everything was going to be okay.

I stood there for a moment, then I turned and sprinted up the stairs.

"Ssssssccccccooooooootttttttttttttttt!" she yelled at the top of her lungs.

I stopped for a second then continued running out the front door without looking back.

As I approached my truck, I took off the backpack and flung it into the bed. Craig was leaning against the driver's side door. I wanted to beat the fuck out of him in the middle of the street, but I was worried my mom called the cops, so I wanted to leave as fast as possible.

"Dude, I'm sor—"
"Fuck you!" I said, cutting him off. "Get the fuck out of here before I beat the living shit out of you!" I yelled as I put a finger in his face. I pushed him off my truck and opened the door.

As I got into my truck, he said, "I am so sorry. I never meant for any of this to happen."

That was the last time I saw Craig.

Thursday, December 12th

After the incident with my mother, I called Steve and arranged the purchase of a teener. I spent the day at his house smoking and hanging out with other random addicts who were purchasing crystal. Around 7:00 a.m., I felt I wore out my welcome, so I said goodbye and walked outside to the sunrise.

I stepped into my truck and drove away aimlessly. I continued driving for the next twelve hours. I made it as far north as Boulder and as far east as DIA. I made pit stops along the way to snort lines in gas station bathrooms, church parking lots, park parking lots, and any other location where human activity level was close to zero. I put over 100 miles onto my odometer.

I drove back to Littleton, and I parked in front of Total. It was 7:00 p.m., and I had to figure out where I was going to reside for the night. I did not want to be around Claire, Kelsey, Jake, Mark, or anyone else, so my options were limited to getting a hotel room or spending the night in my truck. I chose my truck.

I was only a few minutes from Miller's Crossing, and I decided that would be the safest location to set up camp for the night.

When I arrived, I reversed my truck into the ideal location. I picked my backpack off the floor and gently placed it on the seat next to me. I started removing the contents and kept a running tally. There were four used needles, nine charred pieces of tin foil, two light bulbs with crystal residue, two meth pipes, seven tooters, two blackened spoons, five lighters, and one silver serving tray. I put the baggie of what remained of my teener on the top of the pile, the cherry on top of the meth sundae.

I was staring at thirty-three meth-related items, and they were staring back at me. I was dumbstruck by how far I had fallen in such a short time. I was alone, parked in a deserted field on a frigid Colorado December night, with nothing but crystal methamphetamine.

"Fuck it, I might as well go for broke."

I decided to go as low as I possibly could at that moment.

"Eeny, meeny, miny, moe ... and you are the fucking needle that ... is ... it!"

I picked up the winning needle, prepared it and placed it on my lap. Then I dumped a couple rocks into a light bulb, and flicked it with my middle finger to maneuver the meth into the perfect smoking location. I then carved out a line onto a Nirvana *Nevermind* CD case.

My plan was to shoot up, smoke out of the bulb, and snort the line as fast as I could. I had never done all three methods in succession, and contemplated how to conquer the task. I decided going from easy to difficult would be the easiest way to accomplish this feat: snort, smoke then shoot up.

I grabbed a tooter and quickly snorted the line then threw the CD case against the passenger window. Phase one complete. I positioned the flame under the glass and waited until the bulb had a dense, creamy white cloud. I took four enormous hits one after the other, violently coughing on the final hit. I began searching my inner elbow for the ideal location to shoot up. I picked up the needle and slid it into my vein, and then slowly injected the crystal meth into my blood.

I leaned my head against the frosty window and looked up as a snowflake landed on the outside of the window. My breathing eased and I closed my eyes.

....

I could hear "No Rain" by Blind Melon playing through the stereo speakers. For a few seconds, I was unsure if I was alive, dreaming, or dead. I placed my left hand on my right wrist to check for a pulse.

"One-one thousand, two-one thousand, three-one thousand," I whispered.

I was shocked that I had a pulse and was actually still alive.

I slowly started to open my eyes and was unable to focus my vision on anything. I moved my head closer to the dashboard clock and the time displayed 6:24. I had no recollection of what had happened for the seven plus previous hours. I was unsure if I was awake the entire time and could not remember anything or if I had consumed enough meth to render me unconscious.

Shannon Hoon was the lead singer of Blind Melon, and their song "No Rain" was an alternative radio hit in the fall of 1993. Shannon died of a cocaine overdose two years later in October of 1995. He was twenty-eight.

For a few brief moments I thought Shannon was speaking to me from the grave, a sign to get clean, a warning that if I continued to do crystal, I was going to die and end up with the same fate as him.

I became enraged at that notion, and started punching the stereo until my fist and dashboard were splattered with blood. I stopped my assault and looked at my hand; the skin on my knuckles was torn apart and a bloody sliver of plastic was protruding from my flesh.

I was not trying to overdose and die; I just did not care if I did.

Friday, December 13th

I decided that spending another night at Miller's would be ill-advised, so I drove to South Broadway in search of a hotel room. I picked the sleaziest place I could find, the Lucky Me Motel. The deciding factors were the large neon-green shamrock sign, they took cash and there were no cops in the parking lot.

It was a real dive, a place where you would want to bring your own bed sheets and a gun for protection. There was a bullet hole in the wall and bed bugs were jumping all over the bed and floor. The drapes were an off-yellow color from years of sunlight punishment and cigarette smoke. It featured a tiny black-and-white TV with rabbit ears wrapped in tin foil. The volume knob was missing.

I spent the first few hours beating on the TV in an attempt to get reception. My efforts were in vain so I stared at a snowy, white-noise pattern of what I deciphered to be *The People's Court*.

I thought about calling the front desk and complaining in an attempt get a new room with a working TV, but I decided against it because I was worried they would put me in a room worse than the one I had.

I finally gave up on watching TV and started playing solitaire. After cheating to win a game, I stretched on top of the bedcovers and attempted to sleep. I knew sleep was out of the question, but if I could close my eyes for an hour or two, that would almost feel like I slept, and I would consider that a victory.

I rested my head on the bed-bug-riddled pillow at 8:24 a.m. My mind was playing tricks on me, and I did my best to keep my eyes closed. I could not tell if the bed bugs were crawling on my head, or if it was a hallucination; I really did not want to know the answer.

Knock! Knock!

I jumped off the bed onto my feet. My first thought was that it was either the cops or my parents. I wasn't sure what would be worse. I stared at the door in silence hoping whoever it was would go away.

Knock! Knock!

I promptly analyzed the situation and decided if it was the police, they wouldn't knock. They would have kicked the door in with weapons drawn. I ruled them out of the equation. If it was my parents, I probably would have heard my dad yelling or my mom crying. I ruled them out as well.

I cautiously tiptoed to the door and looked through the peep hole. It was hard to focus initially, but as my vision became clear, I saw a female pacing back and forth on the sidewalk. I recognized her as someone staying in a room a few doors down.

After I had checked in, she was smoking a cigarette on a broken lawn chair, and my drug radar instantly picked up that she was a meth addict. She had all the mannerisms of a tweaker: quick, sudden hand movements; constant licking of the lips; nonstop twirling of her hair; and rapid, paranoid eye movement. She could have been twenty or forty, and I would not have been surprised by either one. I wanted to keep my distance from her because she looked like she was deeper into a meth binge than I was. That was saying a lot.

I latched the security chain, and placed my foot a couple inches behind the door then I carefully opened it.

"Hey," she said in her tweaker voice.
"What the fuck do you want?"
"Can I come in?"
"Fuck no!"

I started closing the door, but she barricaded it with her foot.

"Do you have any shit?" she asked.

"Get your fucking foot out of the way!"

"Please let me come in. I'll make it worth your while."

That statement intrigued me, so I went against my better judgment and decided to let her in.

"Don't try anything stupid," I warned her.

"I promise, I won't."

I unlatched the chain and opened the door. She ran inside as I looked outside to ensure she was alone. When I turned around, she was already sitting on the bed.

"I'm Stacy."

"Again, what the fuck do you want?"

"Do you have any meth?"

"No. Now get the fuck out!" I said as I pointed to the door.

She was relentless; her meth radar picked up on me as well, and she knew I had crystal. We continued our *Do you have any?* and *Get the fuck out* conversation for a few more exchanges. She finally jumped off the bed and stood directly in front of me.

"Hook me up and I will fuck the shit out of you!"

She began rubbing the outside of my pants. I looked directly into her eyes as she licked her lips in excitement. I could tell that the thought of fucking me for meth was an enormous turn-on for her, and I bet she was a veteran of fucking for drugs. If you could look past the years of drug abuse and being a meth whore, she probably was rather attractive before she became an addict.

She was over playing games and decided to take control of the situation. She threw me onto the bed and dropped to her knees on the filthy, infested carpet. She spread my legs apart and started rubbing my inner thighs.

"I'll give you the best head you have ever had, and then you can fuck me in the ass. Anything you want," she said while batting her eyelashes.

I already knew fucking her was not a possibility because I was unable to get hard at that moment. Meth was destroying my ability to get an erection to the point that it worked less than half the time. I did want to see how far she would go, though, just to score free crystal.

"Get naked!" I proposed.

She removed her shoes then stood up and removed her pants, shirts, bra, and underwear without hesitation. She was standing in front of the bed completely naked except for her mismatched socks.

"Now what?" she asked.

I stood up and pushed her onto the bed then leaned against the dresser.

"Play with your pussy!" I demanded.
"Whatever the fuck you want me to do, baby!"

She spread her legs, arched her back, and tilted her head onto the pillow. Stacy grabbed her tits then slid her hand over her stomach down to her inner thigh and was inching closer to her vagina. She finally inserted her index and middle finger into her pussy and let out a little moan. She continued masturbating for a few minutes—sometimes fast and hard, sometimes slow and gentle, sometimes loud, and sometimes quiet.

I just sat there watching her masturbate, but my excitement quickly turned to anger. She was willing to fuck a complete stranger for her next high. She was willing to do anything for a bag of crystal, and that disgusted me. I decided I had enough.

"Fucking stop! Stop!" I screamed.

Stacy immediately lifted her head up from the pillow. She still had her fingers inside her vagina.

"Come get your shit," I said dangling her prize baggie of meth in front of her.

She sprung off the bed and grabbed the baggie out of my hand before I had a chance to change my mind. She put on her pants and shirt almost simultaneously then started walking to the door with the bag, bra and shoes in hand. She opened the door and turned back to me.

"Thanks," Stacy said as she blew me a kiss.

I stared at the front door attempting to figure out what had transpired. I decided not to think about it because I would only get depressed. I picked up the foily I was smoking earlier and ignited a lighter to take a hit. I sat down on the wooden chair then put on my headphones.

Winter 1996

It was 11:45 p.m. on Christmas Eve, and I was glaring at the blinking lights and the star perched atop the tree. I was sitting on the couch in the dark with a blanket wrapped around my entire body, attempting to decipher the pattern and timing of the lights. Everyone in the house was long asleep anticipating Christmas morning.

After my third night at the Lucky Me motel, there was police activity in the parking lot, and I was convinced they were there to arrest me for some drug-related violation. Luckily, they were there for a different meth fiend. I knew I had stayed past my welcome, and it was only a matter of time before they would be kicking in my door.

I packed up my belongings and spent the next few days crashing on random couches. The routine grew old very fast, and I knew I had to come up with a plan.

I conceived a story that would fool my mom and gathered the courage to call her. I explained to her that the needles were Craig's (I used him as a scapegoat since he moved to California the day after the needle mishap.) and he peer-pressured me into doing "crystal methamphetamine" three times.

"I didn't like the feeling, and I felt gross each time I did it. I am so sorry! I promise I'll never do it again!"

I conjured a few tears in the process of "coming clean" to her. Crying goes a long way with parents.

"Promise me you will never to it again!" she said.
"I swear on everything that I won't."

I kept that promise for a total of fifty-one hours, my longest sober streak since my first line. I considered that an accomplishment. I also cut back on my meth intake; I was only doing a couple lines a day. I was almost sleeping on a regular schedule, my weight loss stabilized, and my body and mind felt close to normal again—the first time in months.

Before I returned home, I knew I had to acquire presents for my family but my drug fund was quickly vanishing, and I didn't want to spend any remaining money from my savings to purchase presents.

I soon discovered that the best time to shoplift was the few weeks prior to Christmas. Stores were crowded with cheerful Christmas shoppers, and employees were too busy or did not want to bust a shoplifter so close to the holiday; either way, it was a score for me.

My biggest heist was at the electronics department of my local Walmart. I grabbed a shopping cart, placed a thirty-two-inch TV in it, then wheeled the cart directly to the customer service department.

"Hey, I need to return this. It wasn't what I wanted."

After a few mandatory questions and paperwork, I walked away with a few hundred dollars of in-store credit.

There were so many presents under the tree that it was futile to count them, and I stole every present that had a "From Scott" tag on it. I even stole the tape and the tags. The only thing that I purchased was the wrapping paper; I even contemplated stealing a few rolls of that, but I figured walking out with wrapping paper tucked into my pants would be a little noticeable.

As I gazed at the presents, I felt shameful. I could not believe I stole presents I was going to give to my family—including toys for my nephew's first Christmas.

I closed my eyes, dropped my head into my hands, and pressed play on the CD player that sat on the coffee table next to me. "White Christmas" by Bing Crosby began to play.

"Merry fucking Christmas!"

Tuesday, December 31st

A cutting agent is a substance that is used to dilute crystal, cocaine, heroin, or any other powder-based drug with something less expensive than the drug itself. This results in a higher profit margin for the dealer but could result in side effects for the user.

Cutting agents for cocaine can range from flour and artificial sweeteners, to ground-up pieces of drywall. Crystal is usually cut with ephedrine (a stimulant, appetite suppressant, and decongestant), vitamin B12, baking powder, or baking soda. I had heard rumors of crystal being cut with baby laxatives that resulted in the user having to shit immediately after inducing the crystal.

Here is a real-life example: George the crystal dealer buys an 8-ball of crystal for $250. He then goes to the grocery store and purchases a 100-count bottle of vitamin B12 pills for $4.99.

George returns to his double-wide mobile home to start the process of cutting the meth he just purchased. He dumps the crystal into one pile and the B12 into another. He begins chopping up the B12 pills and slowly starts combining them to his pile of crystal.

You might need a calculator for this next part.

Without cutting it, George could separate the 8-ball (3.5 grams) into fourteen quarters (.25 grams) that he could sell for around twenty-five dollars each. If he sold all of them for that price, he would walk away with $350—an extra $100, not a huge profit margin.

Now let's say George cut the meth with the B12 and increased the total weight from 3.5 grams to 5 grams. He would then have twenty quarters and could make a total $500, essentially doubling his initial investment by buying a five-dollar bottle of vitamins.

He could then sell the meth to everyone in the mobile-home park, they would be joyous because they were getting high, and George would be happy because of his significantly improved return on investment. This process is also called getting "stepped on."

There are a few drawbacks to cutting powder:

1. It weakens the strength of the powder, resulting in a product of lower quality, which could anger addicts to the point they would search for a new dealer.
2. When meth is put under heat to be smoked, it turns into a liquid that burns clear. The drug is transparent, and when heat is removed, it hardens back into a solid, forming crystal patterns. When cutting agents are added, the meth will start to burn black. The blacker the residue is after smoking, the more that crystal has been stepped on.
3. The cutting agent can result in countless side effects for the user that include nausea, confusion, cold sweats, irregular heartbeat, damage to internal organs, or in some rare circumstances, death.

I was getting dressed for a New Year's party when I snorted a line, and instantly realized something was wrong. I had horrific, sharp stomach cramps that felt like my stomach was being twisted and pulled apart at the same time. I became paralyzed and dropped to the ground. I was having an adverse effect to the meth.

I curled up into a ball, hoping the pain would diminish. The feeling only intensified to the point where it felt like someone was jabbing a knife into my abdomen. I began sobbing and screaming from the pain.

I decided that making myself vomit might ease the feeling. I started crawling to the bathroom with my knees up into my stomach and my face dragging against the floor. I placed my hands above my head and grabbed onto the carpet to pull myself forward, moving a few inches at a time.

After a thirty minute struggle, I was on the bathroom floor looking up at the toilet bowl. I reached up to grab onto the toilet to pull myself up. After three unsuccessful attempts, I was completely exhausted, and another problem was occurring.

Vomiting was a certainty, but I sensed another issue. I was about to lose control of my bowels. I gave one last fighter's chance at pulling myself up onto the toilet, and when that attempt failed, I just closed my eyes and started vomiting and shitting myself simultaneously.

As I was lying on the cold bathroom tile with vomit on my face and diarrhea in my pants, I heard Dick Clark start the countdown on the TV from my bedroom.

The ball is descending. Listen to the roar of that crowd! In fifteen seconds, it will be 1997. In ten ... nine ... eight ... seven ... six ... five ... four ... three ... two ... one. Happy 1997!

Sunday, January 12th

I knocked twice on Steve's front door and leaned against the siding waiting for the door to open. I had been trying to get a hold of him for the last three days with no success. My crystal supply had run out two days earlier, and I was hoping I could score a teener to hold me over for the next week or so.

I knocked again. I wasn't sure if I was at the right house, so I walked back to the driveway to look for familiar landmarks. Tree with bird feeder: check. Disgusting yellow and orange exterior: check. I was at the correct house.

I wondered if he had gotten busted. The last time I was there he was pointing out a van parked on the street that he was convinced was the DEA. I was getting a bad feeling and started to turn around when the door began to open.

"You're early," Steve said while he continued to open the door.

When the door was completely open, his jaw dropped. I could tell from his expression that he was surprised I was the person standing on his porch. His hand went directly to his gun on his hip. I knew I was in a lot of fucking trouble, and I wanted to run, but I was scared he would shoot me in the back.

"What the fuck are you doing here?"
"Sorry to just show up, but I wanted some shit."

He just shook his head.

"Get the fuck in here!" he said as he pulled me into the hallway and slammed the door behind him.
"Is this a bad time?"
"You stupid motherfucker! Todd is going to be here in ten minutes!"

I got sick to my stomach. I was in deep, deep trouble.

Todd was Steve's main meth supplier who dealt crystal by the pounds, and his transactions were in the thousands of dollars. He was extremely paranoid with a short temper for strangers or unexpected situations, and always traveled with a gang who was armed to the teeth.

Steve escorted me into the kitchen as he bolted the door. I sat down at the table and tried to come up with my next move. My hands were quivering while sweat was dripping off my forehead onto the Scooby-Doo kitchen placemat.

"I can be inside my truck and out of here before he shows up," I pleaded.

He ran up and slammed both fists onto the table. "Are you fucking retarded? He already knows you're here. His guys have been watching my house for hours. If I let you walk out right now, they'd think you're a cop or a fucking rat and probably put a bullet into my fucking head!"

He became so enraged that he flipped the card table that doubled as the kitchen table on its side. Plastic gas station cups, placemats and the salt and pepper shakers went flying across the room.

I dropped my head. I was completely fucked. I was unsure if I wanted to be high or sober for the impending mess. On the sober side, having a clear head would be ideal if the opportunity arose to talk myself out of the situation. On the high side, I would rather have a body full of crystal before taking a few bullets to my head.

In the end, I decided against asking Steve for a line because that would probably put him over the edge, and he would shoot me himself.

I picked up the table and attempted to put all the items back in their places. Steve was frantically pacing back and forth in the entrance hallway. His demeanor pushed me over the edge. I actually thought I was going to die.

Steve finally stopped pacing and sat on a chair next to the front door, anticipating Todd's arrival.

"What the fuck am I going to do?" Steve asked himself.

I folded my arms on the table, closed my eyes, and lowered my head onto my forearms. The room became quite peaceful, and I almost forgot about the dangerous predicament that I had put myself in.

Knock! Knock!

Both our heads sprung up, and we instantly made eye contact like two magnets coming together.

"Don't say a fucking word or do anything fucking stupid!" Steve quietly yelled across the hall.

I was unsure what his definition of "stupid" was, but my plan was to keep my mouth shut and keep my head down. My hope was that Todd would just think I was some random, harmless tweaker, and they would go upstairs to the bedroom to commence their drug transaction.

I watched as Steve started to open the front door then turned away just as I saw the outline of a body. I shut my eyes, closing them as tight as I could and started to slow my breathing. I wanted to be a statue.

I could vaguely hear Steve and Todd exchanging greetings, and then everything got quiet. I started to think I was going to escape the situation unscathed.

Tack, tack. Tack, tack.

I could hear the sound of boots walking along the hardwood hallway floor.

Tack, tack. Tack, tack. Tack, tack.

The sound continued to get louder and closer until I felt someone standing directly over me. I could feel him breathing on the top of my head.

He pulled out the chair that was directly next to me and sat down. He began to tap his fingers against the table one by one. The pace started out slow but increased with each cycle. I could hear each finger on a continuous loop as they landed on the table. Pinky, ring, middle, index; pinky, ring, middle, index; pinky, ring, middle, index; pinky, ring, middle, index. Faster, faster, faster.

I was attempting to remain calm, but I could feel my right hand trembling uncontrollably.

"Hey sport, what is your name?" he finally asked in a calm voice.

I pretended like he was not talking to me, but the tapping got louder.

"Hey! What is your name?" he asked again.
"I'm nobody," I responded with my eyes still closed and my heart pounding.
"Your parents named you 'Nobody'?" he asked as he laughed.

I could hear him softly place a metal object on the table; my guess was that it was a handgun. He then grabbed my hand with his and squeezed it to the point that I thought he was going to break my fingers.

"I'm not going to ask again. What is your fucking name?"
"I'm sorry. I'm Scott."
"Well, that wasn't so hard now was it?"

He released my hand and lightly slapped me on the cheek.

"How about you open your eyes now?" he politely asked me.

My goal was to keep my eyes shut so I wouldn't see if he was going to shoot me in the head. I figured if he was going to pull the trigger, it would have happened right away, so I slowly began to open my eyes—first left, then right.

I was guessing this was the infamous Todd that was sitting across from me. At first glance, this was not a guy I would have pictured as a notorious crystal meth dealer. In fact, he did not even look like a meth user. He was probably in his forties with an average build, had all his teeth and no bags under his eyes, and was dressed like he was going to a job interview or church.

His appearance allowed me to relax for a few brief seconds until I looked down at the table and finally saw what I had suspected was a few inches from my hand, a pistol.

"So what are you doing here, Scott?"
"I just came for a teener."
"Are you sure?" he asked as he inched his fingers closer to the gun.
"I promise." My voice cracked like a teenager beginning puberty.

He began to laugh. "I guess it's just bad timing and a coincidence that you show up a few minutes before I do."

I was speechless.

"What do you think guys? Does Scott have bad timing or what?" he said to his associates.

I turned to my left, and two large men were in the hallway. Steve was nowhere to be seen, and that gave me a grave feeling. I instantly turned my attention back to Todd and the gun directly in front of me. I almost wanted Todd to shoot me; at least it would have been a resolution and put me out of my misery.

"I'm just fucking with you, buddy. Do you want to get out of here?" Todd asked.

I nodded reluctantly.

"Well too fucking bad you stupid motherfucker!" Todd grabbed the gun and put it directly in the middle of my forehead. The metal barrel of the gun was cold against my skin.

I wanted to drop to the ground, piss myself and start begging for forgiveness, but I knew if I did he would kill me right there and toss my lifeless body into a dumpster for a trash man to find. I focused at his finger on the trigger. It was completely still. He looked as if he had been in this exact situation numerous times.

"Give me your fucking wallet!"

I reached into my back pocket and placed it in front of him. He picked it up with his left hand and tossed the various items onto the floor until he found what he was searching for—my driver's license. He positioned it in front of my hand and tilted it back in his direction.

"Is 17012 Fillmore Street your current address?

I nervously nodded, barely moving my head. I was worried if I moved my head too much it might cause Todd to accidently pull the trigger as the barrel was still pressing into my forehead.

"Oh, I know exactly where this house is, lovely area. Who do you live with on Fillmore?"
"My ... my ... my ... par—"
"Spit it out, motherfucker!"
"My parents."

"Your parents you say? I bet they're wonderful people. Do you think they would be heartbroken if you never came home again?"

It took every ounce of strength not to start crying. I knew I had zero control over what would happen. If Todd wanted to kill me, he was going to do it.

I began thinking of happy times growing up: family vacations, birthday parties and holidays. All I wanted was to see my parents one last time and tell them I was sorry and that this was not their fault. My biggest regret was thinking that they might blame themselves for me ending up dead.

He slowly began moving the gun down my forehead, between my eyes, over the bridge of my nose, and stopped at my lips. He started pushing the gun into my mouth, but I clenched my jaw and lips as tight as I could.

"Open your fucking mouth or I am going to break out every fucking tooth in your fucking skull!" Todd demanded.

I figured he could shoot through the back of my head with all my teeth or without them, so if my mouth was open, I would at least have teeth for my funeral. I grudgingly opened my mouth. Todd shoved the gun so far down my throat it initiated a gag reflex, and I almost dry-heaved.

"How does that taste?" he asked as he shoved the barrel farther down my throat.

I did my best not to taste the gun, but when there is a barrel a few inches inside your mouth, you have little choice. I wasn't sure if it was because I was scared shitless or if smoking meth destroyed my taste buds, but I could not taste anything.

"I want you to remember that taste because if I ever see your face again, that will be the last thing you ever taste! Now get the fuck out of here before I change my mind!"

He took the gun out of my mouth and placed it on the table. I grabbed my wallet, jumped out of the chair, and ran to the front door in four huge steps. As I started to turn the doorknob, Todd offered up one piece of advice.

"Hey, Scott."

I promptly turned around.

"See my friend over there? His name is Butch. He's going to follow you home so we know exactly where you live, and if I get as much as a parking ticket in the next few days, he will drive to that house and shoot everyone directly in the fucking head. Have a good night, buddy."

I opened the front door and ran to my truck with such speed that I couldn't stop in time and bounced off the front fender, falling to the pavement. I jumped up and got into my truck to start the drive home.

As I arrived at the first stop sign, I began vomiting onto the passenger seat. After I finished throwing up, I wiped off my face, and I noticed a car in the rearview mirror. I presumed this was Butch.

I made it home a few minutes later and parked in front of my parents' house. Butch stopped two houses up, and as I got out of my truck, he flashed his high beams to acknowledge his presence.

I walked up the driveway and opened the front door. As I walked into the living room, my mom was sitting on the couch with my nephew next to her. She gave me the "shh" sign.

"Try to be quiet so you don't wake him up," she whispered.

I was utterly exhausted, reeked of vomit, and did not want to make small talk.

"Sorry."
"Is everything okay?" she asked.
"Yeah, good night"

I locked the door then made the descent into my room

Wednesday, January 15th

I spent the next few days barricaded in my house, staring out the living room window, looking for any sign of Todd or his henchman. I carried a pocket knife at all times for protection, but I knew that would be little defense against their arsenal. If Todd wanted me dead, there was not a single thing I could do to stop him.

Once I finally came to that realization, I stopped looking out the window, put the knife away, went downstairs to my bed, and closed my eyes. I proceeded to have the best sleep I had had in months.

I awoke and decided I didn't have to worry about Todd anymore. It had been three days since he jammed a pistol down my throat, and I imagined he had done multiple meth deals since then and had long forgotten about me.

I got out of bed, showered, and began a new plan for obtaining more crystal. Steve was out of the question. I was also done with the nickel and dime white-trash dealers Mark and Tony associated with. Their product was usually shit, overpriced, and they were unreliable.

After contemplating my predicament, one practical solution kept coming back to me over and over again.

"I guess I'm going to become a drug dealer," I said as I shrugged my shoulders.

My savings account had been quickly diminishing since I quit the moving job, but I still had a little over $1,400 remaining. I could purchase an ounce of crystal for around $1,200. If I purchased an ounce and didn't cut it with anything, I would have a little over 28 grams of crystal—28.345 grams to be exact. I could snort half of it up my nose, leaving me with 14 grams or 56 quarters. If I sold each of those quarters individually for twenty-five dollars, I would still walk away with a total of $1,400 and a $200 profit. Plus, I would have 14 grams for free.

Maybe being a drug dealer was not such a bad profession.

I figured I would have little problem unloading the twenty-eight grams that I needed to make my initial investment back. There was an endless supply of neighborhood scumbags and druggies who were always looking to get high. If I could get a few of those assholes to purchase crystal from me, they would get their friends to purchase from me, and the rest would start falling like dominoes. After a few weeks, they would be stealing twenty-dollar bills from their family to buy from me.

I also wouldn't have to worry about the larger drug dealers like Steve getting upset because those guys did not want to deal with broke, low-life addicts. I, on the other hand, did not give a fuck.

I picked up the phone and started making calls.

Friday, January 17th

It took me two full days to find someone who could get me the amount of meth I required. I knew it was going to take more than a few phone calls, but I never envisioned it taking multiple days.

All the dealers I knew did not stock that much product on them, but all of them promised they could get it within a few hours. My concern about purchasing from one of those assholes was they would not set up a deal of that size without a kickback for themselves. They would either take money or meth off the top before I touched my product. I also wanted to avoid handing my money to some tweaker who promised to return with the merchandise. There were way too many pitfalls, especially with that amount of money. I had seen Mark make deals like that in the past where his only intention was to steal money from the unsuspecting buyer.

I told everyone that my only stipulation to the deal was that it had to be face-to-face with the dealer, the meth, and the money at the same time. If I was going to get jacked, the guy would have to do it directly in front of me.

Conversations went in circles, and potential deals fell through the cracks. I was starting to feel that I was not going to be able to pull this deal off until Kenny, an old friend called me.

Kenny dated my friend's older sister when I was in high school, and he was of legal drinking age, so he became our high school alcohol connection. I never enjoyed being around the guy, but since he got us booze; it forced me into a friendship with him. I had not talked to him in years, but I was becoming desperate, so I started paging secondary people like Kenny, a guy who, under normal circumstances, I would not talk to.

Kenny called me back within a few minutes, and after some small talk, I told him the main purpose of the call. He paused momentarily.

168

"I know someone who can help you out," Kenny simply stated.

"You do?"

"Yeah, this guy that hangs out at my work."

"Is he legit?"

"Seems like it, but he's Mexican, and he doesn't really speak English."

"Okay, that might be a problem."

"I'm pretty sure he has what you're looking for though."

"Can you ask?"

"Let me call you back in five minutes."

He called back in two.

"Yeah, he said an ounce for $1,100."

"Do you really want to be talking about this over the phone?"

"Why? Is someone else listening?"

"Nevermind."

Details of the transaction were vague. The deal was going down at 1:15 p.m., and it was going to take place where Kenny worked, an independent auto repair shop. Kenny thought the guy's name might be José, but he was not 100 percent sure.

"Okay, I guess that'll work," I said.

I figured I could trust Kenny—well, trust him more than anyone else I had talked to.

As I hung up the phone, it hit me that I was about to become a bonafide crystal meth dealer. That required supplies. The last thing I wanted to do was to return home with an ounce of crystal and be unprepared.

I also realized this was going to be a lot of meth—not something I could hide in my pants pocket. I needed a secure place to store the crystal because I sure as hell did not want to repeat the needle debacle from November.

I grabbed a notebook and created a to-do checklist:

1. Withdraw $1,200 from the bank for the meth and extra start-up costs.
2. Go to a head shop to purchase a scale.
3. Go to a craft store and purchase two-inch Ziploc baggies intended for screws, beads and other shit used for storing crafts.
4. Test to ensure every headlight, tail light and blinker on my truck was in the proper working condition and give my truck a quick wash. I didn't want to be pulled over with an ounce of meth in my glove box. I also believed that if my truck was clean, the odds of me being pulled over would decrease. I had seen enough episodes of *Cops* where they pulled over beat-up cars with bad paint jobs and a broken turn signal.

I completed the checklist before 11:00 a.m. and had almost two hours to kill before my meeting. I briefly contemplated borrowing a gun. I thought this might legitimize my drug-dealer status, but in the end I decided against it. I figured it could cause problems. If "José" wanted to rob me of my $1,100, I would hand it over to him and tell him to have a good day. I did not want to have a gun fight and end up on the local nightly news with a headline that read, "Drug Deal Gone Wrong."

After I nixed the gun idea, I decided to drive to Claire's to have a quick fuck since I had a few spare hours. Because it had been a week since I had seen her, I felt obligated to have a little small talk before I stuck my penis inside of her. She started telling me something about her mom that I completely zoned out. My mind was on the deal, but I nodded intently to illustrate that I was paying attention. After her story was over, I started kissing her neck.

"Were you even listening to me, or did you just come over for a piece of ass?" she said as she slid away from me.
"Of course I was listening. I just missed you. Sorry."

She pondered my answer then climbed on top of me and started kissing my neck. I removed all her clothes and proceeded with the mandatory foreplay before I started fucking her. I quickly finished, laid next to her long enough to catch my breath, then pulled up my pants.

"You are fucking leaving already?"
"Yeah, I have to meet someone."
"Fuck you! Get the fuck out!"
"Thanks babe. I love you."

I kissed her on the forehead and ran toward the door with her completely naked on the bed. Out of the corner of my eye, I saw her flipping me off.

I did not care that she was mad at me, nor did I have time to fix it. I had to be at the auto shop in a half hour and the place was twenty-five minutes away. I did not want to be tardy for my first major drug deal; that would be bad etiquette.

As I was driving, I realized that shooting a load was the best thing I could have done. I felt loose and mentally prepared to do the drug deal.

"Bring it on, José, and please don't try to fuck me over!" I yelled at the top of my lungs.

I arrived at the shop a few minutes early and pulled into a parking spot next to a open garage door. I turned off my truck and sat inside of it, unsure of my next step. My guess was that I couldn't tell the receptionist that I was there for an ounce of crystal. I started to feel anxious. I was looking from side to side for any signal and continued to play drums on the steering wheel, even though the radio was turned off.

Finally, Kenny walked out of the garage and waved me inside. I wiped my sweaty palms on the cloth seat and exited the truck.

"Follow me, man!" he yelled from across the parking lot.

Kenny escorted me through the customer lobby and into a tiny hallway. He stopped at a closed door at the end of the hallway and knocked twice.

"Come in," I heard from the other side of the door.

Kenny opened the door and ushered me into the office. I started walking but almost tripped because my feet felt heavy. By the time I caught my balance, Kenny had shut the door behind me. I was standing in a tiny room with no windows. It had a desk, two old office chairs and a few old car posters hanging on the walls.

A small Mexican man was sitting behind the desk with his arms crossed. This had to be the guy Kenny thought was named José. He gestured for me to sit in the chair directly across from him. There was another Mexican man in the corner behind José. This guy was at least 300 pounds, and wore black sunglasses.

I was about to introduce myself when José turned around and said something in Spanish to the guy in the corner. My Spanish was limited to the semester I took in high school, and they did not mention a cat or what time it was, so I was unable to translate what was being said. The guy in the corner nodded, and José turned back toward me.

"You not cop are you?" he spoke in broken English.
"Fuck no I'm not a cop!" I quickly responded.
"Good, because if you cop, I will have to shoot you."
"If I am a cop, I will shoot myself."

This made him laugh and broke the tension in the room. I removed the wad of hundreds from my front pocket and placed it on the desk.

"Can we get to business?" I asked as I sung "Dopeman" by N.W.A. in my head.

Wednesday, January 29th

I sold out of my first ounce in eight days and returned to José to purchase a second ounce. The process was easier than I could have ever imagined.

My plan to get neighborhood scumbags to purchase from me worked like a charm. The day I returned home with the ounce I separated it into three piles: personal, retail, and samples. I put a few lines in sample baggies and dropped those off to guys I had previously done drugs with and others that I thought could become potential customers. Some of them had never touched powder before, so I had to demonstrate best practices of crystal meth usage.

"Cut out a line then fucking snort it, and please … only do a small amount at first. This stuff is really good, so you won't need a lot."

I emphasized that amount portion of the speech. I did not want to get arrested because some stupid asshole overdosed and died.

Within a few days of dropping off the samples, my pager started buzzing with guys wanting to make a purchase. I spent the next few days driving all over south Denver, dropping off a quarter at someone's house or meeting in a parking lot to discreetly exchange a baggie for cash.

I was selling a lot of meth, making a decent amount of money, and staying constantly high—the ideal situation for a crystal meth addict. The only downside to my newly formed entrepreneurship was that I was becoming exhausted. I was up for days, and when I did sleep, it was for only a few hours until I heard the buzzing of my pager. Being a crystal meth dealer is truly a twenty-four-hour job; when users have money, they want their drugs.

My main concern was that I was going to get sloppy and make a mistake. I kept picturing myself driving to make a deal, forgetting something minor—like using my turn signal when I was changing lanes—and getting pulled over for a minor traffic violation.

On this night, I planned on sleeping, but Mark started blowing up my pager the moment I put my head on the pillow. I contemplated not returning his call, but I knew he would page me every five minutes all night long. I picked up the phone and dialed his number.

"Dude, get up to Total. I know a couple people who are looking," Mark said.
"I can't, man. I've been going for days and need some rest."
"Fuck you, don't be a pussy. I'm trying to make you money, and you're going to say no?"
"I hate your fucking guts. Be there in ten."
"See you soon!"

Jake and Mark had recently gotten hired at Total as cashiers. It was less than a mile from my parents' house. (Unfortunately, it was also less than a mile from Steve's house as well as Mark's parents' house.) They both worked the graveyard shift, and Jake was working on this night.

My plan was to hang out, drink a couple beers, and possibly sell some crystal to potential customers Mark knew. My hunch was the only customers were Mark and Jake.

I arrived a little after midnight, and the party was already in full effect. Jake was working in the front, and the back room was at capacity. Mark and Tony were there along with two girls they were fucking, Shannon and Amy.

The room was the size of a large bathroom and contained a desk, four tall file cabinets, a rolling office chair, and numerous shelves that stored cigarettes, random office supplies, and different-sized cups for coffee and the fountain drink machine. A nine-inch black-and-white TV monitor was on the desk and that provided views of the store from the security camera directly above the cash register.

The walls were covered in posters regarding steps to ensure excellent shopper experience, employee procedures, and Colorado labor laws.

Every time a customer walked into the store, a doorbell rang and Jake had to return to the front to complete a transaction. At that time of night, almost everyone who came into the store was stoned or drunk already, so back-room shenanigans went practically unnoticed. After 2:00 a.m., the bell rang less until it completely stopped.

My hunch was accurate; I was only there to provide crystal for their party. I had two choices: go home and try to sleep or get high. I decided to get high.

I picked up a metal form holder from the desk, and an X-ACTO knife that was in a pen cup. I dumped an entire quarter onto the holder and cut up six lines. I snorted my line, and passed the holder to Tony.

The next hour consisted of doing another quarter of meth, smoking multiple joints, and drinking Old Style. During a crystal break, Jake went up front and grabbed forty one-dollar scratch lottery tickets from the display case. He handed them out to everyone, and we began fiercely scratching them to see if we could turn the tickets into a big winning. The tickets won a total of twenty-seven dollars, so Jake and I had to contribute money to cover the remaining thirteen-dollar balance.

Mark was preparing to ignite another joint when the doorbell rang. I rolled my eyes to the TV screen, expecting to see another drunken teenager stumble through the door to purchase a bag of Cheetos or a lighter.

It wasn't a drunk teenager.

I instantly punched Jake in the shoulder, and he turned his attention to the screen, still laughing from a story Tony was telling. Jake's demeanor quickly shifted to sheer panic.

"Everyone, shut the fuck up!" Jake whispered as loud as he could, prompting everyone to look at the TV screen. The sounds in the room went from laughter to complete silence in mere seconds.

Standing in front of the coffee machine was a Jefferson County police officer. He was refilling his coffee mug that he brought into the store with him.

Jake grabbed a bottle of air freshener and recklessly started waving his arms in every direction, trying to combat the marijuana odor that consumed the room. I was sure this would do little to help. We had been smoking for the last few hours—the entire store probably smelled of weed.

Jake lit up a cigarette and took a couple drags, then put it out on the desk.

"Hide in the corner so he won't be able to see you and lock the door the second I walk out front!" Jake said to everyone.

I could tell he was scared. I was fucking terrified.

Everyone retreated to a corner as Jake walked out. We watched in silence as Jake and the cop had a conversation. The TV did not have audio, so we had no idea what was being said. After a short talk, the cop paid for the coffee and walked back to the coffee counter. He stood there for a moment, then leaned against the counter, sipping on his coffee.

"What the fuck is he doing?" Mark whispered.
"I have no fucking idea," I responded.

My guess was that when he entered the store, he smelled marijuana smoke and called in backup. He was just waiting for them to show up so they could bust in the door and arrest everyone.

The longer I watched the TV without him making a movement, the more I became convinced that he knew we were doing illegal activities in the back room. I did not care about the weed, but getting busted with a couple quarters of meth was a different story. I knew I had to remove as much evidence as possible before the cavalry showed up. Mark was the only person I had confidence in to take on a monumental task.

"You have to split the crystal with me!" I said as I grabbed Mark on the shoulder.
"No fucking way!"
"Yes fucking way!"

I removed the two baggies from my pocket and held them in the palm of my hand.

"What one do you want?"
"I can't snort all of that right now!"
"Eat it! Just force it down your fucking throat!"
"Fuck!" he said as his head dropped.

Mark picked up a baggie, and I took the remaining one. I opened the baggie and placed it against my lips, preparing to dump the contents into my mouth. Mark followed my lead.

I was already getting sick, just thinking about swallowing that much meth. I took one final glance at the TV screen, hoping the cop would exit the store. No such luck.

I began the countdown. "3 … 2 … 1!"

I nodded my head, and we both dumped the meth into our mouth. I turned away from Mark. I did not want to see his reaction because I knew that would make my experience worse.

I closed my eyes and started swallowing the larger rocks so they would not have the opportunity to stick to my teeth. I gagged and almost spit out the remaining powder, but I forged through the urge. I began swallowing the powder in tiny amounts, one after one, with each swallow becoming tougher than the last. It felt like I was swallowing a mixture of baby powder, baking soda, and corroded batteries. I can easily say it was the worst taste I had ever experienced.

I finally finished and opened my eyes to see Mark sitting on the floor. He dejectedly pointed to the monitor. I turned around toward the TV and the cop was no longer in the store.

"Fuck!" I yelled at the top of my lungs as I punched the file cabinet.

Saturday, February 1st

I turned onto Fillmore and parked a few houses down the street from my house so I could inspect myself in the rearview mirror. I felt beyond strung out. I had heavy black bags under my eyes from being awake the last four days, commonly referred to as raccoon eyes in the meth world. My face was oily, and it looked like I had a thick layer of grease on top of my skin. I was starting to develop a severe meth sore, but luckily my facial hair was concealing a portion of the enormous mound.

I smiled to examine my teeth, but the normally simple task was difficult. After I got my mouth open, I began rubbing my gums and blood started dripping onto my teeth. I was expecting that result, so I was not shocked. I used my tongue to clean off my teeth and spit the blood onto the floor between my legs.

As I examined my face closer, I noticed something I had not seen before. It appeared that the inner segment of my eye socket collapsed in. There was a definite indentation on my left eye that was not reciprocated on my right. It looked like the tissue behind my skin just eroded. I pushed my pinky into the chasm, and it felt like my finger was sliding into my eye socket. I removed my finger, deciding that I did not want to know what was happening.

On a scale of one to ten, I would say I was a negative two. This was the worst I had ever looked. I picked up a water bottle and started splashing water on my face, hoping I could move from the negative to at least a zero.

After a few attempts I gave up. It wasn't doing anything, and I was getting water everywhere. I did not want to show up at home looking like a fucking tweaker who just pissed his pants. My hope was that since I had not slept in four days my hallucinations were tricking me into thinking that I looked worse than I did.

I drove the final few hundred feet to my house. I got out of my truck and proceeded to make the walk of shame to the front door.

I opened the door and took only a few steps before I noticed my mom sitting at the dining room table enjoying her morning cup of coffee. My nephew was sleeping in a crib in the living room. I would have done anything to sneak past her and go into my room without having a conversation.

She turned around when she heard the door open and began inspecting me head to toe, looking for any sign that I was high. I was confident I could deceive her for a short period, but the longer I stood there exposed, the greater those chances diminished.

I was far enough away that it would be difficult for her to see the exact condition of my face. I did my best to stand my ground, stay out of direct light, and keep my distance.

"Where have you been?" she finally asked. I knew if she did not start yelling at me, I was safe for the moment, and I passed her initial test.
"Me, Jake, and a few other guys were up all night playing Nintendo 64."

That sounded like a believable lie.

"Are you high?" she asked.
"No, of course not!"
"You are not lying to me, are you?"
"Yes, I promise. I'm just fucking tired. Sorry for saying the f-word. I just lost track of time and I'm exhausted."

She nodded to display her approval. I realized I was a better actor than I thought. I resumed my walk to the stairs when she asked me one final question.

"Hey, can you watch him while I run to the store? I need to grab some milk and a couple other things."

That was the last thing I wanted to hear.

"I was really hoping I could just get some sleep. Can't you just take him?"

"I think you can at least watch your nephew for twenty minutes. Is that so much to ask?"

The only excuse I could say to get out of this situation was to tell her that I was high, and since that was not happening, I reluctantly agreed.

"Okay, please hurry."

She gave me a quick tutorial on the fundamentals of changing a diaper and was out the front door.

This was the first time I had ever been alone with him; in fact, this was the first time I had ever been alone with an infant. I was intimidated, and downright scared of the situation.

I watched him roll back and forth in the crib and was unsure what I was supposed to do. My eyes felt like they were burning, and I dearly wanted to close them, but I was worried if that happened, I would be asleep for hours or even days.

I decided to sing him a lullaby in some off chance he would fall asleep, but I couldn't remember a single one. I sang the first song I could think of, "Brain Stew" by Green Day. He either did not like my singing or Green Day because as I finished, he started to cry. It was in short and quiet bursts at first and then quickly escalated to an uncontrollable, ear-piercing volume.

Waa! Waa! Waa!

I attempted to give him a bottle; he didn't take it. I attempted to give him a pacifier; he threw it. I did the "shh" sign over my lips, but he turned away from me. He would not stop.

"Please be quiet, buddy," I pleaded with him.

Waa! Waa! Waa!

I felt completely helpless and finally gave up and threw in the towel. I rolled onto the floor and crawled into a fetal position, plugging my ears in an attempt to filter out the high-pitched crying.

Waa! Waa! Waa! Waa! Waa! Waa!

Saturday, February 8th

Mark's new girlfriend, Kimmy invited me to a party in the mountain town of Evergreen. She was a beautiful, blonde girl and out of Mark's league—they were not even playing the same sport. I figured she was using Mark for free drugs.

"These are mountain kids who have rich parents and love to get fucked up. I guarantee you'll sell a bunch of shit," Kimmy told me over the phone.

I was concerned that Kimmy sounded overenthusiastic about me making drug money off her friends. I knew if I arrived at the party and it was a façade to steal all my drugs and money, I would have to take whatever beating they wanted to hand out. I contemplated the situation, deciding the reward outweighed the risk, and prepared ten individual quarters of meth. That amount was a little excessive, but I would rather have extra than sell out and have to make a trip down the mountain for more.

I picked up Mark and drove Bear Creek Road past the town of Morrison and Red Rocks into the beautiful mountain meadows that featured a series of hairpin turns with steep drops on the other side of the guard rail.

"Make sure I don't get too drunk because I do not want to drive this after ten beers and a few shots," I said to Mark.
"I'll try to remember."

After about forty-five minutes of driving mountain roads past one-stop-sign towns, we arrived in downtown Evergreen. I located the gas station, and pulled into the parking lot. Kimmy and her friend ran out of the store and jumped into my truck.

"This is Beth. She's awesome!" Kimmy proclaimed.

After everyone jammed into the cab and we had proper introductions, Kimmy then began giving me directions to the party. Evergreen mountain roads were confusing due to the lack of streetlights, paved roads, and the only visible landmarks being Evergreen trees. I guessed that was probably where the town's name originated.

"Take a left at the fence post!" Kimmy shouted.

I felt like we were driving in circles, but from out of nowhere a mansion appeared on the side of the mountain.

"There it is!"

I drove up the long driveway, and stopped at the walkway.

"You guys can get out here. I'll find a place to park and meet you inside," I said.

I turned around and drove to the bottom of the driveway until I found an ideal spot to park. I carefully reversed my truck onto the dirt shoulder next to the pavement about three car lengths in front of the closest car. I always made sure I was prepared for a fast getaway. You never knew when shit was going to go down and you would have to flee a sticky situation. The last thing I wanted was to have to maneuver out of a tight spot with a bunch of methed-out tweakers in hot pursuit.

From the bottom of the driveway, it was about a five-minute walk to the entrance of the enormous house that had a four-car garage. I walked past the perfectly landscaped trees and shrubs until I made it to the oversized, custom front doors. I had no idea who lived there and wasn't sure if I should walk in or knock. I decided knocking would be the courteous thing to do.

I knocked and waited. I turned around and took in the breathtaking, picture-perfect view. The house sat on the top of a mountain, and it seemed like the next closest building was miles away on the opposite mountain. I looked up at the clear sky, and the amazingly bright stars.

I had forgotten I was waiting for someone to answer the door. I put my ear against the door and could hear "Gin and Juice" by Snoop Dogg blaring from the other side, so I assumed no one could hear the knocking.

I slowly turned the doorknob, and pushed open the door. The volume of the music and smell of weed instantly hit me in the face.

I walked into the foyer and saw a couple on a couch in the living room. They were practically about to have sex, and I did not want to interrupt them, so I tiptoed across the hardwood floor. My efforts were in vain, and the guy stopped his activities to glare at me.

"Sorry," I offered up.
"Fuck you, cocksucker!"

I resumed walking toward the source of the music. After walking through an empty hallway, I located the living room and the party. The room was full of guys a few years out of high school still wearing their letterman's jackets. I wanted to walk up and start pummeling one of them in the face, but since I was outnumbered something like fifty to two, I decided to hold off on that. I figured the next best thing was to sell them my drugs and make a profit off the fuckers.

"Hey guys, this is Scott. The guy I was telling you about," Kimmy said as I approached the group she was talking to.

I walked into the group and introduced myself to everyone. Without hesitation, the dumbest-looking guy opened his mouth. I didn't catch his name, but he looked like a fucking Troy to me.

"Do you think you could sell us some crystal meth?" Troy asked.

I almost laughed in his face but figured he might take that as an insult and beat the shit out of me as retribution for making fun of his intelligence. I did not want to make big Troy angry.

"Yeah, but we should go somewhere a little more private," I said. "Follow me."

....

After a few hours, multiple lines, several beers, and a couple more drug deals, I was invited into a different spare bedroom. Kimmy and a few other people wanted to smoke meth, and I figured it was the perfect opportunity to sell my remaining crystal.

When I entered the room, I immediately got a different vibe. The guys in the room were not the clean-cut, white mountain kids I had been selling to all night. The mountain kids wanted to get drunk then do a line to sober up enough to get their dick hard so they could fuck some drunk girl. They were amateurs, dabblers, and rookies.

These guys had the presence of serious tweakers, and that scared the shit out of me. They looked like they were high-strung and unstable, a mirror image of myself.

There were three of them. The two bigger guys sat on the edge of the bed and just stared at me as I entered the room. The smaller one was sitting on a chair next to a nightstand that had an enormous mound of meth on its wooden surface. He was sliding the crystal back and forth with a razor blade. He did not divert his attention away from the powder when I entered the room. I knew he was in charge, so I attempted to greet him.

"Hey, I'm Scott," I said as I offered my hand for a handshake.

He did not look up from the powder and continued transferring the meth from one pile to another.

"So I hear you are trying to sell some fucking dope?" he asked as he slammed the blade on the nightstand.

"Um …" I was unsure how to answer that question. I looked over at Kimmy to get some assistance, but she was too high to sense the gravity of the situation.

"I came to this party with the intention of selling a lot of crystal, and some fucking cracker said you were the dope dealer. Is that true?"

"Well, Kimmy told me that a couple of her friends wanted some, so I brought a little extra. I had no intention of stealing your customers." I was trying to redirect some of the responsibility to Kimmy, hoping it would protect me from a severe beating.

"You punk ass little motherfucker, do you think you're some sort of fucking drug dealer?" He lifted up his shirt to reveal a handgun without looking away from the nightstand and the powder.

I knew I could have sprinted to the door before he could remove his gun, but Kimmy would be left alone with some pissed-off meth dealers. I would have felt bad about that, but she was the one who introduced me to these guys, so it was partially her fault.

I decided I would give one last plea before I bolted for the door.

"Dude, I am so sorry. I had no idea that you were here. I would have never stepped on your toes."

He finally looked up at me. After a few extremely tense moments, he finally smiled.

"I'm just fucking with you, man. Don't go pissing yourself," he said, laughing.

He stood up and I extended my hand again, but he pushed it away and gave me a hug. As he was patting my back and laughing, I expected him to shove a knife into my spine.

"I'm Brad. Nice to meet you!"

I spent the next few hours doing a lot of crystal with Brad and talking about the drug business.

Around 4:00 a.m., the party was dying down, and I went to the upstairs patio with Beth. I was trying to fuck her, but I wasn't making any headway. I sensed she was flirting with me just enough for me to give her more meth. I had to give her props; she knew how to work it. Flirt enough to look interested, ensuring a constant flow of free drugs.

I looked down to the courtyard and saw Brad standing there with his crew and a few guys from the party. He pulled out his gun, and pointed it straight up to the sky.

I immediately thought he was going to shoot someone over a drug deal gone wrong.

BANG! BANG! BANG!

I jumped back from the noise of the gunshots and almost tripped over a patio chair. That was the first time I had ever heard a gunshot in real life, and it was a lot louder than I expected.

Everyone in the backyard scattered. Some people ran into the house while others ran into the forest. Brad made his point. I was not sure what it was, but he made it.

"I think it's time to leave. Go find Kimmy and Mark and meet me at the truck," I said as I walked past Beth.

Tuesday, February 11th

I was in my room attempting to take a power nap when I received a 911 page from Mark. When most people added a 911 after their code on a page it meant it was an emergency. When Mark added a 911 code, it usually meant he needed a ride or drugs, or both. I decided to ignore the page and curled up into a ball at the foot of my bed.

Bzzzzzzzz.

I picked up my pager again and looked at the screen.

697 911 911 911

That page concerned me. Mark's code was 697, but he inserted three 911s after his code. Mark never sent more than one 911 in a page. I reached down and moved my hand across the floor until I felt the cordless phone. I turned it on and dialed Crazy's number.

Before the first ring cycle completed Mark answered.

"Dude, you need to come get me right now!" he screamed into the receiver.
"Calm down! What the fuck is going on?"
"Please, just come pick me up right fucking now! I need to get the fuck out of here ASAP." He sounded desperate.
"Okay, I'm leaving right now. Be there in ten."

I had a feeling Mark was in serious trouble, so I immediately began getting ready. I put on my shoes, tied the laces, and snorted a line. If shit was going down, I did not want to show up sober.

I was in my truck in less than two minutes, and if not for the red light at Kipling, I would have arrived in the time I promised. I turned into the apartment complex and began searching for a spot to park when I noticed a silhouette running toward my truck. It was

189

hard to decipher, but I guessed the figure was Mark, and he was in full Carl Lewis sprint mode. I expected figures to appear chasing him.

I did not want to continue driving in Mark's direction, so I slammed on my brakes and put the truck in reverse. I quickly completed an 180-degree maneuver that positioned my back tire onto the sidewalk.

I unlocked the passenger door, pushed it open, and watched the tiny figure become larger and larger in the side mirror. Mark leaped into my truck and simultaneously slammed the passenger door.

"Go! Go! Go! Get the fuck out of here!" he screamed.

It was not the time for questions, so I smashed the gas pedal and sped out of the apartment complex. My attention was in the rearview mirror, and I did not notice the stop sign I ran and the Volkswagen Jetta I almost sideswiped in the process. The driver of the Jetta swerved and slammed on his brakes to avoid me. I gave him a courtesy wave.

I turned into the first possible neighborhood, driving in excess of 50 mph on residential streets, jumping over speed bumps and the sensation like we were on two wheels around corners. I kept one eye on the road to avoid pedestrians and parked cars and the other fixated on the mirror to ensure no one was following us.

After a few minutes of the NASCAR-style driving, my adrenaline succumbed to curiosity. I turned off my lights and coasted to a complete stop in front of a small park. I kept my truck running in case Mark's pursuers discovered our location.

"What the fuck is going on?"
"I fucked up."
"What did you do?"
"Crazy told me his family was coming over, and that's when I called you. I began packing up all my shit when some guy walked

through the front door. He was yelling then just started punching me in the face. I slipped away from him and jumped over the patio fence and hid in a bush until I saw you pull into the parking lot."

With the help of a streetlight, I finally noticed Mark had scratches on his face, a fat lip, and dried blood under his nose.

"Why was he hitting you?"
"I really fucked up this time," Mark remorsefully said.
"You said that already! How exactly did you fuck up?"
"Crazy is broke. His checking and savings are gone. We spent everything on meth. He doesn't have money to pay rent."

I had a suspicion that Mark was stealing from Crazy's bank account, but to spend every dollar of a paraplegic senior citizen's disability for meth was about as low as anyone could get—even for Mark.

"How much?"
"I don't know, thousands."
"Thousands?"
"Three, four, five thousand. Maybe more. I don't know. It's all gone. Everything."
"God damn it, Mark!" I yelled as I slammed my fist against the dashboard.
"Will you just drive?" he asked.

I never saw Crazy again.

Friday, February 14th

Brad contacted me to gauge my interest in a meth deal: he knew a guy that was looking to unload a large amount of meth at discount prices. Under normal circumstances I wouldn't have done a deal like that, but I was in somewhat of a pinch.

José was nowhere to be found. I had been calling Kenny every day for two weeks, but he had not seen him, and no one in the shop knew where he was; he vanished. I was really hoping that he got deported back to Mexico or was in jail, but my instincts told me he was murdered during a meth deal gone wrong and buried somewhere in the mountains. Either way, I was out a drug dealer.

I was also getting low on inventory—personal and business. I had about an 8-ball remaining, and I knew that would not make it past the weekend. I went against my better judgment and reluctantly told Brad I would give this guy a call to potentially set up a deal.

"And remember, this is a friend of a friend of a friend so if you get jacked, it's not on me. And if you get hooked up, you owe me," Brad said in his normal smart-ass tone.
"Thanks for the reassurance."

I hung up and looked at the piece of notebook paper that I scribbled his name and number down on.

"Rex," I said as I tapped the pen against the paper.

I did not like the name. I did not know a single person named Rex nor could I think of a single person I'd ever heard of named Rex, but that did not stop my growing hatred for the name. It reminded me of Todd because they were both one syllable names, and that gave me a bad feeling. I then remember my name contained only one syllable. I decided I was overanalyzing the situation.

I came up with four possible outcomes:

1. I give him money, he gives me the correct amount of high-quality crystal, and we start a marvelous dealer/buyer relationship. That would be considered the perfect drug deal, but that is more of a fairy tale than reality.
2. I give him the money, he gives me average crystal that is good enough to sell, and I make my money back.
3. I give him the money, he gives me a bag full of baby powder and ephedrine, and I curse him the entire drive home, vowing revenge on the fucking cocksucker.
4. I give him the money, he takes it and shoots me in the head, and I end up in a shallow grave next to José— well, not literally next to him. That would be the worst-case scenario.

I picked up the phone then slowly dialed the number. Rex picked up after the second ring. We started in on small talk: the weather, how horrible the Nuggets were playing, how great the Avalanche were playing. Small talk was mandatory on phone calls that involved a drug deal. I was not sure why, but I guess it is good etiquette and a precaution in case either of us were undercover cops or if the phone was tapped. After a few minutes, we started in on the purpose of the call, and it quickly escalated into amount, pricing and quality.

"How good is it?" I asked.
"I'll take the Pepsi fucking challenge with any Denver shit, any day of the fucking week," he confidently responded.

Quoting *Pulp Fiction* definitely scored a couple street-cred points with me. We continued talking until we worked out the remaining details of the deal. I negotiated a final price of $1,050 for an ounce of crystal meth, fifty dollars less than what José charged.

"Go to the Burger King in Edgewater. Call me when you get there."

I hung up and immediately paged Mark, Tony, and Jake because I did not want to make a major meth deal with a new dealer alone. I anxiously waited for the phone to ring. After ten minutes I knew there would not be a return call, and I was going to be on my own for the meeting.

"Fuck, let's go make a deal!" I said with fake enthusiasm as I clapped my hands.

I grabbed the money and my keys and stuffed them both into my pocket. As I was walking down the driveway to my truck, Claire paged me, and I remembered it was Valentine's Day. I had promised her that I was going to take her to dinner and a movie.

I knew that returning the page would initiate a fight, so I decided to ignore it and call her back the following day with a lie as to why I stood her up. I would have endless opportunities for forgiveness, but if I bailed on this deal, I would have been cursing myself for weeks.

It took me forty minutes to drive to Burger King. I parked next to the pay phone, grabbed some change out of the ashtray, then walked to the phone to make the call.

"Okay. Go west on 26th until—"
"Are you not meeting me here?" I said, interrupting Rex.
"Fuck no!"

He then started to give me detailed directions to a parking lot where he wanted to meet. I did not feel safe about making a meth deal in a random lot; there were too many factors that could go wrong, especially for me.

"I'm not doing a deal in some fucking parking lot. Meet me here!" I demanded.
"Fuck no. Cops drive by that place every few minutes. Meet me at my location or the deal's off."
"Fuck, let me go grab something to write down the directions."

I then drove until I saw the apartment complex alley where I was supposed to meet him. I turned off my headlights and started scanning the lot left to right, back to front. The only thing I could see was a stray cat searching for food in a dumpster.

Rex appeared from out of nowhere and was suddenly standing at my driver's side window.

"Yo man, let me see the money," Rex said while he was investigating the cab of my truck. He was high as fuck.
"Jump in."
"No fucking way!"

He removed a baggie from his coat pocket and placed it at the base of the window. It looked like a lot more than an ounce.

"I'm not buying anything without trying it first."
"This is the best shit in town," he responded.

I was about to respond when headlights drove past the alley. That put us more on edge.

"Do you want this shit, man? Or else I'm bouncing," he said, looking back to the street.

I grudgingly pulled the money out of my pocket, and we exchanged the money and meth in unison. I placed the baggie on the passenger seat and turned back to Rex, but he disappeared behind a dumpster as quickly as he appeared.

That was not a neighborhood where I wanted to be hanging out with an ounce of meth, so I put the truck in drive and pressed on the gas.

I navigated the steering wheel with my left hand and placed a tooter into the bag with my right. At the first stop sign, I leaned over and snorted a line. I instantly knew it was not meth and was just a worthless bag of powder that resembled meth—most likely ephedrine with other cutting agents mixed in.

"Fuck! Fuck! Fuck!" I screamed as I punched the windshield.

Friday, February 21st

I was still upset from the drug fiasco with Rex because I went against my gut feeling. I knew that I should have driven away, but I didn't. I handed Rex the money, and he handed me a bag of mysterious white powder.

The entire drive home that night I was trying to convince myself that the line I snorted was a bad section of the bag, and the meth and the cutting agents were not properly mixed. When I arrived home, I thoroughly mixed up the contents of the bag and dumped a quarter into the crease of a tin foil pipe to give the product an appropriate test. I flicked the lighter and inhaled a massive cloud of smoke as it came off the foil. I instantly started coughing and almost puked from the taste. I spit on the floor to get the aftertaste out of my mouth.

I already knew what color the mystery powder was going to leave on the foil, but I had to have one final confirmation that I was swindled. It was completely black.

"Of course!" I said as I transformed the tin foil into a paper airplane and threw it across the room.

I came to the conclusion that the entire contents of the bag were most likely cutting agents and completely worthless. I thought I was smarter than that. I thought I would never end up on the wrong side of a drug deal.

I drove the streets of Edgewater a few times, hoping I would run into Rex. I wasn't exactly sure what action I would take if I did, but I at least wanted the opportunity. After a few days of searching for him, I finally gave up, and I decided he would not be dumb enough to be walking the streets in the same location where he just pulled off a thousand dollar heist. If I was in his shoes, I would have gotten a shit ton of meth and booze and locked myself in someone's basement for a few weeks.

I was almost out of money. I had a minuscule amount of actual crystal and an ounce of imitation stuff. I could try to sell the imitation stuff to novice meth users, but experienced users would immediately know this was shit meth and wouldn't pay a penny for it. I put it away for a rainy day in case I ever got in a predicament.

I decided not to dwell on the situation any longer. I wanted to get high with my last remnants of crystal. I picked up Mark and Tony, and we spent the next few hours cruising Colfax Avenue, the street that was made famous in the novel *On the Road* by Jack Kerouac.

Colfax featured bums, prostitutes, and burnt-out drug users, as well as hotels that charge hourly rates and a liquor store or bar every few hundred feet. Almost every street corner had a homeless person holding a cardboard sign begging for money. I could have probably yelled out the window that I needed drugs and dealers would come running from every direction. Those were my people and it felt more like home than home did.

We would turn down alleys and strategically park behind dumpsters out of the view of passing cars. Before the truck came to a complete stop, Mark already had the flame under the light bulb and the tooter in his mouth. We would take a couple hits, put the meth supplies in the glove box, and continue our journey east on Colfax toward downtown Denver.

Around midnight, we finished the last trace of crystal.

"That's it!" Tony said as he threw the bulb out of the window, shattering the glass onto the alley cement.

I made a U-turn and began the depressing journey west back to Lakewood.

As I drove, panic began to set in. That was the first time as a meth addict that I was out of money and out of meth, and it was a frightening feeling. I started thinking about how I was going to get high on Monday or Tuesday or Wednesday. My biggest fear was being one of those addicts you see on a drug documentary that live day to day begging or stealing for crystal, or like Jim Carroll from *The Basketball Diaries* who sucked dicks in shady bathroom stalls in exchange for heroin. I would rob some old lady's purse before I got that desperate.

"Can you drive me to John's house?" Mark asked out of nowhere.

John was Mark's stepdad and was ironically an undercover narcotics agent for Denver County. Yes, I did say "undercover narcotics agent."

"Fuck that. I am not going anywhere close to that house!" I quickly responded.
"He's working, and nobody is there. I just need to grab a couple of my things. Five minutes tops."
"Promise me you are not going to do anything illegal.
"I promise. I have to grab some clothes and some other shit."
"Don't fucking believe him!" Tony chimed in.

Being anywhere close to the house of a narcotics agent while being extremely high was not on my priority list, but since we no longer had any drugs, I felt a little safer about it. I decided to trust Mark.

"You have five fucking minutes."
"Thanks, man."

After about ten minutes of driving, we arrived in a secluded, upscale neighborhood next to a golf course.

"Park over there."
"You better not be lying to me," I said.
"I'm not! Everything will be fine. I'll be back in a few." Mark jumped out of the truck and ran down the long, dark driveway.

Tony and I sat in silence, anticipating Mark's return.

"What if he breaks into John's secret stash and brings back the most primo shit in the state?" Tony asked.

"You're a fucking idiot."

I was kind of thinking the exact same thing, but I was not dumb enough to say it. I was certain if John had drugs, they would be locked up and as secure as his gun collection.

After about ten minutes, Mark was running back up the driveway with a backpack hauled over his shoulder.

"Let's get out of here!" Mark said, out of breath as he slammed the door shut.

"What is in the bag?" Tony asked.

"Just some of my stuff."

"Where are we going?" I asked.

"Motel 6 on sixth. I'm going to stay there tonight."

"What? Where the fuck did you get money?" I asked.

"I had some of my money there."

"Did you steal money?"

"No! It's my money, so technically it's not stealing."

"Fuck, Mark!" I yelled.

I knew he was fucking lying, and once John discovered he was robbed, he would quickly figure out Mark was the perpetrator. The police would be on the lookout for him, and I didn't want to be anywhere around when they found him.

I broke multiple traffic laws on the short drive to Motel 6 and pulled into a parking spot away from the front lobby. I didn't want to be seen with Mark or Tony.

"Can you still give me a ride in the morning?" Tony asked as he turned back to me.

"I'll be here at ten sharp—be ready. And don't forget to page me the room number."

He nodded, gave me a peace sign, then slammed the door. I drove away as fast as I arrived.

Saturday, February 22nd

I knew there was no possible way I could sleep, so I kicked off my shoes and attempted to relax on my bed. I was there for less than a minute before I became restless and began moving. I picked up the TV remote and started channel surfing, not staying on any one channel for more than a few seconds.

I stumbled upon an infomercial for the Psychic Friends Network, and I became mesmerized by it.

I think that everyone watching this show can benefit from talking to a psychic. Meet psychic to the stars Linda Georgian.

I began to wonder if this shit actually worked. The longer I watched, the more I became convinced it did. I wanted to know if I was going to end up in jail or be murdered. I picked up the phone and started dialling the 800 number but stopped halfway into it. I came to my senses and decided $4.99 a minute was not worth hearing some bullshit artist tell me a bunch of made up lies I wanted to hear. I resumed my channel surfing.

Around 5:00 a.m. I entered meth limbo, the period where the crystal high had passed, but a long way from sober and being able to sleep. It plays tricks on you because when you feel like you can finally sleep, you get excited and lie down. Then you close your eyes, and that is when you feel your heart rate pounding. This is the reminder that your brain might be ready for sleep, but your heart and body are not.

It was at this stage that I remembered that I still had the bogus meth I had purchased from Rex. I convinced myself that his meth required time to settle, like a fine wine. I got out of bed, grabbed the powder and started forming a line.

I snorted the line, and it instantly burned my nostrils. I cursed myself for snorting that fucking powder and started punching my head in attempt to offset the immediate headache. It didn't work. I decided to get up and prepare for the day.

....

I arrived at Motel 6 around 9:45 a.m. I walked up the staircase to the second floor then along the hallway, stepping over various items of trash until I reached their room.

Knock, knock. Knock, knock.

There was no response. I put my ear against the door, but I could only hear the TV. I began to think Tony gave me the wrong room number until I heard a commotion that sounded like someone fell off the bed.

"Who's there?" Mark yelled from the other side of the door.
"It's Scott, fucker! Open the fucking door. It's freezing."

Mark unlocked the deadbolt, unlatched the chain, and opened the door. The room was a fucking disaster. Beer cans were scattered all over the two twin beds and floor. Cigarette butts were on the dresser, nightstand, and on top of the TV. There was a random girl in the bed with Mark, and her clothes were at the foot of the bed. It looked like they had occupied the room for ten days, not ten hours. I did not want to set foot in that fucking place.

"Where is Tony?" I asked.
"Getting ready," Mark said, pointing to the bathroom.

I maneuvered around the trash to the bathroom and banged on the door.

"Let's go!" I yelled.
"Give me five minutes," Tony quickly responded.

I pushed a few empty beer cans onto the floor and nervously sat down on the edge of the bed. I had an uneasy feeling about being in the room that Mark paid for with stolen money. I glanced back at the other bed and Mark and the random chick were on the verge of fucking, so I turned my attention to the Saturday morning cartoons on the TV.

BAM, BAM, BAM!

I looked away from Bugs Bunny to the front door. It sounded like whoever was on the other side wanted to kick the door down. I assumed it was the Lakewood Police Department. I prepared myself for policemen pointing shotguns in my face and drug sniffing dogs biting at my ankles.

"Open this door right now, Mark!" a voice yelled from the other side of the door.

I turned back to Mark, and his face was pale white. I cautiously pushed myself off the bed and walked to the front door. I moved my head to the peephole and squinted through it onto the balcony.

"It's fucking John!" I whispered.

Mark already knew it was John.

John was a short, stocky bald guy in his early forties that looked more like an insurance salesman than a undercover narcotics agent, but I guess that was the perfect cover.

"Fuck! What do I do?" I whispered to Mark.

Mark helplessly shrugged his shoulders.

I looked back out the peephole and examined the surroundings. John was alone. I decided I could push him back against the balcony railing, and that would give me a small enough window to outrun him in a foot race down the hallway. I played high school football and figured I could perform a swim move around that fat fuck.

"This is your last warning, Mark! I'm going to call the police if this door does not open in thirty seconds!" John yelled. He sounded deadly serious.

Without saying a word, I opened the door and attempted to slither around John, but my plan was instantly thwarted. He was bigger and stronger than he looked and pushed me back into the room with one hand before I could plant both feet onto the hallway cement.

"Sit down, Scott!" he shouted at me.

John directed Mark and the random girl to sit on one bed and Tony and myself to sit on the other. One by one he instructed us to put our hands on the wall and spread our legs while he feverishly frisked us. He found a tiny amount of weed on Mark that he threw into the trash can. I knew he was searching for crystal, but fortunately for us, we were in the midst of a dry spell.

After he finished frisking everyone, John stood directly in front of Mark.

"Did either of these guys assist you last night?" John asked Mark while he pointed at Tony and me.

I was anticipating Mark to open his mouth and tell John that we were accomplices. Mark was a horrible liar, and I assumed he would crack under the pressure of facing possible criminal charges.

"No," Mark said to my amazement.
"Are you sure, Mark?"

It sounded like John was trying to give Mark every opportunity to implicate Tony or myself in the crime.

"No, I was alone. I went into your house alone. They had no idea what I was planning to do or what I did," Mark said somberly without moving his head.

"You guys have five seconds to get the fuck out!" John shouted to Tony, the random girl, and me.

I jumped off the bed, exited the room, and started speed walking down the hallway. When we made it to the parking lot, the random girl pulled a couple twenties out of her bra and looked up at us.

"Do you guys want to go to Denny's?" she asked.
"I guess I could go for some French toast," I responded, knowing I could not take a single bite.

Sunday, March 9th

I awoke after sleeping for what felt like the better part of several weeks. I reached over and pulled down the blanket that I had tacked above my blinds to prevent sunlight from beaming into my room. I was unsure what day it was; it really didn't matter.

My body ached, and my muscles had atrophied from spending twenty hours a day in bed. I also noticed a stain on my sheets, and I crossed my fingers that it was from the night sweats I was having and not due to the fact that I pissed my bed. Either one would not have surprised me though.

I picked up the TV remote, and my right hand began trembling so forcefully my mattress started moving. I grabbed my right wrist with my left hand in hopes I could impede the shaking. This started an internal struggle between both limbs. The tighter I grabbed, the more it trembled. My bed felt like one of those vibrating beds that you find in a sleazy motel.

I attributed this condition to my meth withdrawal, and I finally gave up, knowing that there was only one thing that would help subdue the tremors.

After a few more hours of lying in bed and watching TV, I finally decided to get up. I showered, got dressed, and started flipping the pages of my phone book, looking for people I could unload the bogus meth on.

I wanted to keep my distance from Tony and Mark because I knew John was watching us after the Motel 6 episode. Mark received a second-degree burglary charge, a class 3 felony in the state of Colorado. I also figured selling bogus meth with me was not something Mark would do, considering he was possibly facing a few years in the state penitentiary.

I started paging the meth users that I considered the worst of the worst. These guys would snort gunpowder if you told them it would get them high. I was hoping they would be so strung out they would not notice how bad that shit was.

I sat on the couch, waiting for the phone to ring, picking it up every few minutes to ensure there was a dial tone. The phone remained silent.

I kicked the end table in frustration, propelling the phone into the air and dislodging the batteries when it landed. I quickly realized that someone might be calling and would get a busy signal, so I dropped to my knees and grabbed the batteries to replace them in the headset.

I looked up at the mound of white powder that was sitting on my bed. It confirmed my failures as a drug dealer. For a brief moment, I contemplated flushing it down the toilet and entering a rehab facility. I decided I was delusional.

I dedicated myself to selling that fucking powder. I searched deeper into my phone book and sent out a second round of pages to a few lesser-known associates.

After minutes of waiting, the phone finally rang.

"Hello?" I asked.
"Is this Scott?"

....

I was parked in front of a pleasant suburban two-story house in Littleton a couple blocks from Columbine High School. Under normal circumstances, selling meth to a complete stranger was terrifying, but I figured this powder didn't contain a grain of crystal meth, so I could not be charged with an actual crime.

I had no recollection of meeting this guy, but apparently I met him at the party in Evergreen.

I walked up the sidewalk and knocked on the door then waited for an answer. The door swung open, and a short, skinny, pimple-faced teenager stood in front of me. He barely looked like he was a teenager.

"Hey, Scott! How are you doing?"
"Hey man, I'm good."
"Come on in." He said as he gestured me into the house.

I followed him down the hallway, past framed family pictures hanging on the walls, and stopped at one particular picture.

"Where was this?" I said, pointing to it.
"Oh, that was last summer at Disneyland. My parents, little sister, and grandparents went out to California for a week. It was a blast."
"Mickey Mouse huh?"
"Yeah, fuck that mouse!" he said, laughing.

We continued walking down the hallway until we arrived at his room. He had posters of Michael Jordan and John Elway hanging on the walls and various sports trophies on his bookshelf.

"What grade are you in?" I asked.
"I'm a senior."

I realized he could not be older than eighteen. For the first time, my conscience started getting the best of me. I felt despicable. I had no qualms about destroying my life, but I no longer wanted to contribute to destroying someone else's.

I was about to call off the deal when he naively asked, "Is it $100 a quarter?"

I nodded my head yes.

After I made the deal, I drove straight to Brad's house and purchased two quarters with the money I had just acquired. There was a large group of people hanging out, so I fabricated a lie to leave. I did not want to share any of my meth with anyone else.

I drove my neighborhood until I stumbled upon the elementary school where I attended sixth grade. That was where I first met Jake, where I had my first girlfriend, where I got in my first fight, and where I got third place in the 100-yard dash on field day.

I exited my truck and started walking past the basketball court toward the playground, kicking pebbles along the way. I stopped at the monkey bars and attempted to make my way across, but I made it only three bars before dropping to the gravel below.

I continued walking until I reached the swing set and sat in the middle plastic swing. I grabbed the rusty chain, pushed myself as far back as possible, and lifted my feet off the ground. The wind across my face felt wonderful, and it reminded me of being a carefree kid. I didn't want the ride to stop because once I touched the ground, reality would recommence. I was a broke, jobless, crystal meth addicted teenage degenerate.

The ride stopped, and I decided play time was over. I got off the swing and walked toward a park bench on the outskirts of the playground. I placed my backpack next to me and removed various meth-related items, including a needle.

I injected the crystal meth then slid off the bench onto the gravel below with the needle still inserted in my arm. I remained there for what felt like an hour but was probably closer to five minutes. A dog barking in the distance startled me, and I knew it was time to move on.

I pulled the needle out of my arm and tossed it sidearm-style underneath the monkey bars as the sun began setting over the mountains to the west.

Friday, March 14th

Tony and I were stuck in I-25 morning traffic a few miles north of Colorado Springs. It was bumper-to-bumper traffic, and every time I stepped on the gas I almost instantly slammed on the brakes to avoid a rear-end collision.

Tony had called me and asked if I would do him a favor by picking up a friend who was getting released from the county jail. In exchange, he promised he would get me high and the friend would give me an additional quarter once I dropped her off at home. I was still jobless and crystal-less, so this was a no-brainer.

Colorado Springs is located seventy miles south of Denver, and on a good day the drive can be completed in a little over an hour; it was not one of those days. The radio reported an accident a few miles ahead of us that created the traffic stalemate.

"What did she do?" I asked out of curiosity.
"Who?"
"The girl we're going to pick up."
"Oh, Jessica? I think it was for a warrant or something. It wasn't for anything major—I know that."
"How long has she been in for?"
"A few days maybe, I'm not sure."
"You don't know what she did or how long she's been in for?"

Tony squared his shoulders in my direction. "What the fuck do you care? Are you her fucking lawyer?"
"I guess I don't."

I assumed she did something worse than a warrant, and Tony didn't want to talk about it. I just decided to drop the subject before we started throwing punches at each other on the interstate.

After a long, tense pause, traffic started moving, and minutes after that, we approached our exit. About twenty minutes later, we located the jail. I turned into the parking lot and drove toward the back of the lot.

"Why the fuck are you parking all the way in the back?" Tony asked.
"I don't want to be anywhere close to the front entrance."
"Well, this makes us look guilty as fuck! Who parks in the back of the parking lot unless they're guilty of something?"
"Newsflash asshole: we are fucking guilty of a lot of shit!"
"Well, you don't have to advertise it by parking so far away."
"Fine."

Nothing will bring out paranoia like being high, parked at a jail, and surrounded by cops. I turned around, returned to the front of the lot, and parked in a spot I felt would satisfy Tony.

I had an uneasy feeling. I was waiting for a K-9 unit to walk in front of my truck and for the drug-sniffing dog to start barking. The cops would then search my truck, and arrest us on the spot. On the bright side, it would have been a short walk to the jail.

"Where is she?" I timidly asked.
"I don't know. Let me go look."
"You are not leaving me here alone."
"Be back in a second."

Tony jumped out of my truck, but stopped as he was about to shut the door. He removed a tooter and an empty baggie from his jacket and placed them under the floor mats.

"I almost went in with these!" he said, laughing.

He slammed the door and started skipping to the front of the building. I was now alone, and any drug charges would fall solely on me. I knew Tony would rather hitchhike back to Denver than share the culpability.

I glanced down at the clock. It had been over ten minutes since Tony left, and I was starting to get worried. I looked back up, and two cops were slowly walking directly in front of the truck. I waved as they passed.

I was watching the cops on the sidewalk when the passenger door flung open. Tony stood there with a smile.

"Look who I found!" Tony said.

....

Jessica was the female version of Steve: tall, skinny (probably weighing no more than ninety pounds), missing a few teeth, and at certain angles it appeared she was missing chunks of hair.

I did not want to be around her because I could sense she was trouble. I wanted to drop her off, get my meth, and drive back to Denver, never returning to this fucking shithole of a town.

"Do you want to do me another favor?" Jessica asked.
"No! Maybe, what?"
"After we go to my place, will you drive me to my boyfriend's? It's like ten minutes from my house."

That was tweaker talk. I would have bet anything it was at least forty-five minutes away.

"No, I have to get back to Denver. I have shit to do."
"What the fuck do you have to do?" Tony asked, quickly joining the conversation.
"What if I give you another quarter?"
"Fine." I reluctantly accepted the offer.

When we arrived at the apartment, Jessica ran into the bedroom, and I sat on the couch next to Tony. The tiny, one-bedroom apartment was in complete disarray. It smelled like the litter box had not been changed in months. The kitchen trash can was

214

overflowing onto the floor. There were ashtrays filled with cigarette butts everywhere, and I really mean they were everywhere—on the coffee table, under the coffee table, next to the couch, on top of the TV, and at least five in the kitchen.

An elderly woman was sitting at the kitchen table, and I presumed she was Jessica's mom. She was reading a *People* magazine and chain-smoking. She had on a robe that exposed a partial view of her breasts.

There also was a little kid who was probably not more than five years old sitting in front of the TV watching cartoons and playing with Legos. He looked at Tony and me then turned his attention back to the TV. He seemed to be accustomed to having strange men in the living room. When Jessica opened the bedroom door, the little kid jumped to his feet and ran in her direction.

"I missed you Mommy!" he screamed as he gave her a hug.

She quickly returned the hug then looked up at us.

"Are you guys ready to go?"
"No, Mommy! You can't leave again," he cried louder.
"I promise I'll be back in ten minutes, baby."
"No! No! No!"

The kid had probably heard that promise countless times and knew she was not coming back in ten minutes.

"Mommy!" he screamed as he clinched her leg harder.

The look on her face told me she was getting annoyed. She reached down and removed the kid's arms from around her leg and dropped him on the hallway floor. He started screaming at the top of his lungs.

"Mom, can you please fucking take care of him? I have to go meet Doug."

215

"Yeah," the old lady in the kitchen responded without diverting her eyes from the magazine.

"Let's go!" she said without glancing back to her child.

"I changed my mind. I have to go." I said as I pushed myself off the couch. I decided I would rather drive home with a quarter less of crystal than spend another minute with this heartless bitch.

"What?" Tony and Jessica asked simultaneously.

I walked out of the apartment and ran down the stairwell to my truck.

....

I dropped Tony off when we arrived back in Denver and drove straight to my elementary school, parking in the same location I did last time I was there. I casually started walking toward the playground, but I picked up the pace to a jog after my first twenty steps. By the time I made it to the basketball court, I was in a full sprint.

I tripped on a crack in the sidewalk but stopped the fall with my hands, scraping them in the process. They were bloody and small pebbles were embedded under my skin. I regained my balance and continued running.

When I arrived at the monkey bars, I dropped to my knees and began throwing gravel into the air, searching for the needle I discarded there. I used my hands as shovels and tossed the gravel and sand mixture fiercely over my shoulder, creating a large dust cloud. I continued digging until I reached solid dirt, then I would move a few feet to the right and initiate the process again.

I paused for a moment to look down at my hands; they were bright red and covered with a combination of blood, dirt, and sand. A small piece of glass was lodged in my palm. I pulled it out and safely placed it into my pocket.

I continued digging, but it became apparent that the needle was no longer there. I finally gave up after displacing half the gravel beneath the monkey bars. I formed a tiny mound of gravel, rested my head on it, and began crying as the sun set behind the mountains.

Tuesday, March 18th

After I left the playground, I vowed to myself to stop doing crystal. I went home and gathered up all my supplies: light bulbs, tooters, miscellaneous pieces of tin foil, baggies, and any other random instrument that I used to snort, smoke, shoot, or sell crystal meth with.

I put everything into two plastic grocery bags and threw them in a 7-Eleven dumpster. It felt like I just dropped my life into the trash. I figured my life for the last eight months was the equivalent of the bottom of a dumpster.

I returned home and sat on the edge of my bed, looking around my meth-less room, contemplating my next move. I then remembered a conversation I had about drugs and life with this tweaker at a party.

He grew up in a middle-class family, graduated from college, became a high school teacher, got married to his college sweetheart, and had two beautiful children.

"I only smoked weed throughout high school and a little in college, but no powders until I went to a bachelor party about five years ago. I think I was thirty-seven. I snorted a line, then another, then another. I started out doing it on the weekend like every other cliché drug user starts out. Then it turned into a Thursday night until Sunday morning thing, and before I knew it, I was doing lines off my desk before class," he told me before snorting a line.

Eventually everything collapsed. He got fired, and his wife kicked him out of the house and filed for a divorce.

Tweakers are naturally thieves and liars, so my general rule was to believe only about half of what they said, but this guy seemed honest and genuine. He gave me the impression that he was trustworthy.

"I'm still searching for my wrecking point," he said.

"What's a wrecking point?"

"It's the point where you come to the realization that you can't get any lower. The point where shit gets beyond fucked up. It could come after doing drugs for one day, one month, or one year, but it will eventually happen. It could be caused by going to jail or a loss of a job or a major health issue or a friend overdosing or your family leaving you! It's a significant event that will make you see the light and quit being a fucking junkie!"

"Are you close?" I curiously asked.

He paused and snorted another line.

"I thought my wrecking point would be when my wife left me. It wasn't. Then I thought it would be when I lost custody of my kids, but it wasn't. I think I'm getting close. I feel like I'm at rock bottom: no family, no kids, no job, no money, and no place to live. I'm as low as I can go, but on the bright side it can only go up from here. … It has to," he said with nervous laughter.

"I hope so for both of us."

"Thank you for the lines," he said as he shook my hand and politely exited the room.

I heard through a friend of a friend of a friend that he put a gun in his mouth, pulled the trigger and splattered his skull and brain matter against the wall. I guess he finally realized his wrecking point.

....

My sobriety lasted only two days until Brad called and asked six simple words.

"Do you want to get high?"

"When and where?" I responded.

I began putting my shoes on before I heard the stipulation. There are no free lunches in the drug world—especially with Brad—and that instance was no exception. His regular delivery driver flaked, and he needed someone to drive him throughout the Denver metro area to make his crystal deliveries.

"I will get you high all day and give you gas money, and after we make the last stop, I'll give you a quarter."
"Deal," I said before he could amend his offer.

I would have done it to get high all day, but since he was offering cash and extra meth, it was a definite yes. I finished tying my shoes and ran out of my house, skipping in excitement.

When I arrived at Brad's parents' house, he was already standing on the sidewalk waiting for me. He got into my truck, sat down, and examined the contents of his backpack to ensure he had not forgotten any of the supplies he needed for the day. He removed numerous premeasured baggies of meth, a scale, a roll of cash, a notebook, and the final item … a gun. The gun made me nervous, really fucking nervous. I was about to renege on the deal until he explained why the gun was necessary.

"It creates a façade. If these fuckers know I'm packing, the likelihood of shit getting fucked up goes down because these people don't want to get shot over a few hundred dollars. It makes the operation smoother and safer for all sides involved. Fuck, it's not even loaded."

His explanation put my worries at bay, and I started driving. He opened the notebook and skimmed through pages until he located the page that had the directions.

"Aurora is our first delivery," he said as he pointed east.

The first delivery was to an average suburban housewife and mother of three. She was in her thirties and had an average body and a pretty face. I would not have suspected her as an addict. Her two oldest kids were at school, but the youngest was asleep in a crib about ten feet from the dining room table where the deal was taking place.

I think she was worried I was there.

"I only do meth as a dietary supplement. I'm still trying to get rid of this baby weight. It seems like it is the only thing that works for me," she explained to me.
I wanted to call bullshit but figured that would be bad dealer etiquette, so I politely nodded. "Of course, I completely understand."

Our next three stops were to the stereotypical meth users and abusers. One was a guy who worked overnights stocking shelves at a grocery store, another was a kid my age who looked like he had been up for weeks, and the last one of the three was a couple in their late twenties requiring it for a road trip to California. They reminded me of the couple you would see on *Cops* who were involved in repeated domestic disputes.

We were dealing meth for hours, and I was getting antsy. Dealing drugs at a small-time level is a mundane process: small talk, product testing, negotiations, exchange of money and drugs, doing the newly purchased drugs, more small talk, and the final goodbyes.

We also made constant trips to convenience stores. I kept a running tally, and we stopped six times: twice for Newports, twice for Mountain Dew, once for a lighter, and once so Brad could make a phone call. I began to understand why Brad's original driver bailed and almost wished I would have done the same.

"Final stop!" Brad proclaimed.
"Thank fucking god!"

Our last stop was at a run-down mobile home park in the town of Sheridan. That was the first time I had been inside a mobile home, and it was everything I had pictured. The interior featured fake wood paneling with mismatched couches covered in hideous upholstery from the 1970s. There was also a stench coming from underneath the floorboards; I envisioned a family of dead, rotting raccoons.

"Hi. I'm Megan," the woman on the couch said to me.

Megan resided in the mobile home and to put it nicely, she was disgusting. It was not often that you run across an overweight tweaker. She was probably pushing 200 pounds, but her face had the characteristics of a well-seasoned meth addict. When she raised her arms, the enormous mounds of fat under her triceps swayed side to side. The dress she was wearing was too small, and it revealed more of her ass and tits than I wanted to see.

Brad and Megan followed the normal protocol for the deal, and after they finished, Brad excused himself to go to the bathroom.

"Do you have a girlfriend?" she asked.
"No." I was not sure why I said no, because the thought of doing anything with her sexually almost made me vomit on the table. I guess I was just programmed to say no to that question.
"Here is my number. Call me sometime if you want to hang out and get high," she said as she wrote her number on a piece of paper and slid it across the table to me.

I took the paper and placed it in my pocket. It was never a bad idea to have the number of a fellow addict.

"Thanks. Could you tell Brad I'll be in my truck?" I said as I excused myself and walked to the front door.

Spring 1997

I spent the night doing crystal alone, listening to music, and rearranging my room. I moved my bed and dresser into three different places, but I was unsatisfied with the new layouts, so I moved everything back into its original position.

Around 3:30 a.m. I contemplated paging Mark or Jake to see if they wanted to get high, but I decided against it. I was becoming more and more antisocial and preferred smoking crystal by myself than in the company of others. I grabbed a coloring book, a red and green crayon, and I started coloring instead. I did my best to stay within the lines, but it was not an easy task with my hand tremors.

I concluded my coloring project, and flipped through the pages to view my finished work. I had started coloring fifteen different pages but did not complete a single one.

"Maybe next time."

I placed the book under my bed and proceeded upstairs to grab a Coke from the fridge.

As I walked into the kitchen, I saw my mom sitting at the table drinking coffee and reading the *Denver Post*. I remembered that she was taking the day off.

"Good morning. Anything interesting in the paper?" I asked.
"Morning. No, not really."
"Cool."
"Hey, do you want to get lunch? Maybe go to a movie after?" she asked.

I scoured my brain for an answer.

"I'd love to, but I have an interview at eleven. They said it might take an hour or two, so can I have a raincheck?"

"Yes, of course, honey. Good luck," she said as she turned her attention back to the paper.

She was doing her best to smile. I could tell she knew I was lying, and that is why I did not get any follow-up questions about the interview. I think deep down she knew I was back on drugs, but she was ashamed to admit it. She did not want to face the fact that her youngest child was a crystal methamphetamine addict and slowly killing himself.

"I love you," she said.
"Love you too, Mom."

I looked back at her for a few more moments of awkward silence then closed the fridge door and walked back to the stairs without saying another word.

....

I hustled as fast as I could to leave my house. I showered, put on my interview attire, and ran out of the house when I heard my mom walk up into her room.

I drove straight to Total to put five dollars in my empty tank. I was holding the gas nozzle watching the digital display increase when I heard a voice.

"Scott?" a guy yelled at me from the opposite side of the gas pump.

I didn't recognize the voice, and that always worried me. It could have been someone I owed money to, someone I owed crystal to; a boyfriend of a girl I fucked, or someone who purchased bunk acid from Mark and wanted revenge. I could probably list about twenty other different scenarios, but I think you get the point. I clenched my fist in preparation for a fight and turned around to see who was calling my name.

"Scott, I thought that was fucking you!"

It was fucking Steve. I had not seen or heard from him since the night I had a handgun in my mouth at his kitchen table. I wanted to pull the nozzle out and spray gasoline over his entire body then toss a match on him.

"Hey, I just wanted to say sorry for everything that happened. The entire situation was beyond my control," he said, extending his hand.

I did not know how to react to his gesture, so I kept my hand on the nozzle. He retracted his hand and continued talking.

"A couple weeks after that shit happened at my house I got raided by the fucking DEA! I was crashed out after being up for ten days and woke up to a shotgun up my fucking nostril."
"Yeah?"
"Yeah, and the funny thing is that I was completely out of shit. I sold my last 8-ball the day before they kicked in my door! They raided my house when I was completely, fucking dry! They only found a few ounces of marijuana."
"Funny," I said sarcastically. He did not pick up on my social cues.
"You're telling me! What are the fucking odds? They knew I was a dealer, and they wanted me to rat out Todd, but I told them to fuck off. After a few hours, they had no choice but to release me with a few misdemeanor charges."

I didn't believe any of his story. I went to his house on at least twenty different occasions, and he always had a significant amount of crystal. I didn't see him allowing his stash to dwindle to nothing. I just didn't believe it.

"After that shit happened, I said fuck the cops and fuck this town! I'm sick of all the bullshit, so we are moving. Grand Junction, here we come!"

I found it hard to believe the DEA would be that incompetent and raid his house when he was completely meth-less. It didn't add up to me. They probably spent days upon days, weeks upon weeks, watching his every movement. They knew who came and went; they knew when he had large quantities and when he was running low. I bet they waited until he had his peak amount of crystal, and that's when they commenced the raid.

I pictured Steve sobering up and realizing he was facing multiple felonies and years in jail. He probably cut a deal with the DA to spare himself heavy prison time. He was a spineless piece of shit, and that was the only way I could see him a free man.

"Take care, Scott," he said as he gave me a hug like we were friends.

He walked past the gas pump back to his station wagon with his wife and two little kids. His girl waved at me holding a stuffed rabbit, and I waved back.

....

I drove around Littleton searching for a location to get high. I picked Clement Park. The park has numerous football fields, four baseball fields, soccer fields, a couple playgrounds, a reservoir, and paths that encompassed the entire park. It is fucking enormous.

I parked in a lot north of the baseball fields and examined the area. The parking lot was practically empty except for a few cars spread sporadically throughout it. A father and son were flying a kite on one of the soccer fields, but besides them, the park seemed empty.

I turned off my truck, grabbed my backpack, and started walking toward the baseball fields. As I got closer, I became nostalgic. I remembered playing Little League there. It felt like a lifetime ago, even though it was only six or seven years at the most.

I walked down the embankment to one of the fields, through the dugout, and onto home plate. I kicked up dirt and dug into the batter's box then threw off my backpack and took a few imaginary swings. I pretended connecting with a fastball that flew deep into

227

left field. I ran full speed up the first-base line until I reached the hole where the first base bag would be placed. I turned around and dejectedly walked back to home plate to retrieve my backpack.

I made my way up the main concourse that had a concession stand with a bathroom in the back of the building. I opened the bathroom door and bent down to make sure all the stalls were empty. They were. I walked into the last one and locked the door behind me.

I sat on the frigid, metal toilet seat and removed drug paraphernalia, placing everything on my lap. I took a few hits and then I relaxed, leaning back against the toilet tank.

I was about to start round two when I heard footsteps walk into the bathroom. The noise startled me, and I dropped the bulb onto the concrete floor. It bounced off the concrete, and I reached down and grabbed it before it hit the floor again.

"What was that, Daddy?" a kid's voice asked.

I jammed everything into my backpack and quickly ran out of the stall.

"Howdy!" I said as I rushed out of the bathroom.

Wednesday, April 2nd

After I left the bathroom, I ran the entire distance back to my truck; it felt like a marathon. I tossed my backpack onto the passenger seat and drove out of the parking lot as fast as I could. I was on the road for about five minutes when I got that feeling you get when you forget something—like the feeling you forgot to turn off the stove or lock the front door.

I reached into my jean pockets and pulled both of them inside out. My heart leaped into my throat. My baggie of meth was missing. My precious was missing! I recklessly crossed two lanes of traffic and turned into an Albertson's parking lot. I jumped out of my truck before it came to a complete stop and frantically searched every remaining pocket.

My front pockets were empty. My back pockets were empty. I dumped the entire contents of my backpack on the seat of my truck, and the baggie was not mixed in with my drug paraphernalia.

"Fuck! Fuck! Fuck!" I yelled as I banged my fists on the hood. I jumped back into my truck and sped back to Clement Park. I was in a race against time, and I decided to disregard every traffic law; my missing crystal outweighed the safety of other drivers.

I approached a parking spot at such a high speed that I skidded across the asphalt until my front tires jumped the curb and stopped on the grass. The smell of burnt rubber was in the air as I started my sprint back to the bathroom.

I was running across a football field when I spotted something glimmering in the sunlight off in the distance. I made a beeline in that direction. As I got closer to the glistening object, I became more convinced this was my baggie of crystal. I was about to find my pot of gold under the rainbow.

I was sprinting at such a high speed that as I approached the baggie, I overshot my intended target. I performed a midair flailing, acrobatic tumble and landed directly on my chin with such an impact that I felt like I gave myself a concussion. I remained lying on the grass with my eyes closed.

I inhaled the smell of freshly cut grass with the blades tickling my face. I already knew what I was running for was not my bag of crystal; it was a mirage, a glass of water in a barren desert.

I slowly opened my eyes and looked up at the shining object. It was a cellophane from a cigarette package. I picked it up and threw it, but the wind blew it directly back into my face.

I recommenced the journey to the bathroom, already conceding defeat.

··········

I returned home from Clement Park with no crystal meth, no money, no job, and zero means to obtain any in the foreseeable future. I was starting to see a pattern.

I began preparing myself for the inevitable crystal methamphetamine withdrawals.

Day 1 (Typical Stage): This was routine, and it felt like a normal, drug-filled day. I was still high from my excursion in the park bathroom. I was worried about my lack of crystal, but also confident that everything would work itself out. I had been in this situation before.

Day 3 (Fatigue Stage): I was feeling extreme fatigue, so I slept for two days. Trips to the bathroom were exhausting, and walking short distances resulted in breathing difficulties and had me gasping for air. The few hours I was awake were consumed by making calls and sending out pages searching for my next fix.

Day 5 (Craving Stage): I had slept a better part of 120 hours over the course of five days, and I could not sleep any longer. I attempted to resume a regular eating schedule, but my stomach could not hold down food, and I vomited after almost every meal.

My crystal methamphetamine cravings were as high as they had ever been. I developed a sensation in my left wrist and began scratching at it. Without noticing, I had scratched my skin completely raw. The area was red and exposed, but I continued digging my nails into my open flesh because it was the only release that would satisfy my cravings.

Day 7 (Paranoia Stage): Mark, Jake, and Tony were not returning my calls, and I pictured them getting high together, and laughing at me. I tore apart my room, searching for any baggies that I might have hidden from myself in case of emergencies, but I found nothing. I cursed everyone and everything and punched at anything within striking distance. That resulted in multiple holes in the drywall and bloody knuckles.

Day 8 (Scheming Stage): I wrote down every possibility of obtaining crystal. I considered cooking up a batch, but I did not have the knowledge or expertise to do so. I would have probably just blown up my parents' house. I considered selling or trading my truck for crystal, but the title was in my dad's name, so that was not a possibility. I strolled through the neighborhood at night peeking into parked cars, looking for anything of value that I could steal. I did not know how to remove a car stereo and found only worthless items like clothing and coins in ashtrays. I snuck into my parents' room while my dad was taking a nap and ransacked his wallet, but I only found a couple dollar bills.

Day 9 (I will do whatever the fuck it takes to get High Stage): A few hours from Thursday and ten days without crystal: over that period, I experienced every emotion—aggression, anxiety, depression, embarrassment, frustration, hatred, hopelessness, hostility, loneliness, regret, and remorse. This was the first time in my life that I had truly experienced drug withdrawals.

I picked up a piece of paper that I found in my wallet a few days earlier. It was something I was avoiding at all costs, but I knew this was a guaranteed way to get high. It was Megan's phone number, the woman who lived in the mobile home. I dialed the numbers into the keypad and pressed call. She picked up after the third ring, and I began explaining who I was, but she stopped me.

"Oh, I remember who you are, sweetie. What's going on?"

Under normal circumstances, I would not have just come out and asked someone if they had meth and wanted to get me high for free. It was bad etiquette, but I wanted to spend the least amount of time talking to her as possible, so I got directly to the point.

"Do you have any crystal?"
"Yeah, come on over," she said.

....

I stood in front of the door and analyzed the Catch-22 situation. I needed to get high, but I did not want to get high with Megan, but she was the only person that could get me high, so if I did not knock on this door, I would not get high.

I finally knocked on the door, foreseeing my impending fate. The door opened, and I got my first glimpse of Megan. She looked older, less attractive, and fatter than I remembered. The last time I saw her I had been smoking crystal all day, so I almost certainly had the meth equivalent of beer goggles on.

"Come on inside."

We sat at the kitchen table and talked for a few minutes until she reached for a metal box, which she placed on the table. She opened it and removed two bags, each containing at least a half gram of meth. My mouth started salivating.

Megan loaded a bulb, and we passed it back and forth until it was cashed. She loaded another one, and we repeated the process. I closed my eyes, leaned back in the chair, and exhaled. I finally felt normal again. It was a pleasant feeling.

What I felt next was not a pleasant feeling. Megan was rubbing my crotch. I mean, if I wanted to fuck her, it would be a pleasant feeling, but I didn't want to fuck her. I also was pretty certain I couldn't get hard, and even if I could, the sight of her naked would probably make me limp.

"Fuck the shit out of me and I will get you high all night!"

She said the magic words. I stood up and followed her into the bedroom.

Thursday, April 3rd

I heard "Black" by Pearl Jam playing on the cheap transistor radio from the living room. I slowly opened my eyes to see the wood paneling and a used condom on the carpet. I felt ill.

"I need some fresh air," I said as I got off her stain-covered mattress. She remained on the bed with her saggy boobs resting on her beer belly.

I walked through the hallway, stepping over dirty dishes, broken toys, and various items of trash. I made it to the front door and was about to turn the doorknob when I glanced over to the kitchen table and spotted her stash box between two Keystone Light cans.

I knew it contained at least a half gram if not more, and there was no way I could pass up that opportunity. I justified it as hazard pay for the previous night's work and the possibility of catching an STD.

I lunged at the table, grabbed the box, and then secured it above my forearm like a running back carrying a football. I flung the door open and was running at full speed down the driveway within a few seconds. I even hurdled a Big Wheel without missing a step.

As I approached my truck, I removed my keys from my pocket and began flipping through them until I found the right one. I unlocked the door and turned back to have one final look at the mobile home.

Megan was standing on the jury-rigged patio wielding a steak knife in the air.

"I'm going to kill you, you fucking cocksucker!"
"Thanks, you stupid cunt!" I yelled as I waved the box in the air.

I got into my truck, turned on the ignition, and slammed my foot on the gas. The rear end of my truck fishtailed on the loose gravel in the process. I glanced into the rearview mirror and Megan was halfway up the driveway. She threw the knife as I drove away.

....

I had plans to hang out with Claire the night before, but Megan and her free crystal meth sidetracked me. I decided it was better late than never. I drove onto I-25 and began weaving in and out of traffic reaching almost triple-digit speeds. I finally slowed down after I nearly rear-ended a family in a minivan.

When I arrived at Claire's house, I snorted a line then ran across the yard to the back door. I knocked twice then opened the door and entered her room—sixteen hours late.

Claire was sitting on the edge of the bed in pajamas with her head in her hands.

"Where were you last night?" she said without looking up.
"I'm so sorry, babe. I was so tired I just passed out."
"Do you swear?"
"Yes! I swear on everything," I said with sincerity.
"That's really funny because I went to your house last night and your truck wasn't there. Your mom said you were not there either. In fact, she said she hadn't seen you in a few hours."

It never crossed my mind that she would drive to my house. I needed a lie, but I had a major problem. I was high as fuck, and my brain wasn't working properly to make up something on the spot.

"I was with Jake. He was going through some shit last night. It's a long story, and I don't want to bore you."

She remained silent for a few moments then slowly got off the bed and walked toward me until she was directly in front of me.

"How fucking stupid do you think I am? I've heard all the rumors! I've heard all the girls you've fucked!"

"I promise I have never cheated on you!" I said as I laughed.

I always laugh when I get anxious; it is not a good personal trait to have, especially when your girlfriend is accusing you of cheating.

"How many girls have you fucked since we've been together?" she asked as she started punching my chest.

"No one! I swear I have only been with you!" I grabbed her hand and pushed it away from me.

"You're a fucking liar, Scott!" she screamed at the top of her lungs. I was worried the neighbors would hear and call the police.

"Can we sit down and talk please?"

"Let's see …," she said as she closed both fists, preparing for a countdown on her fingers. "I know for a fact that you've fucked Kelsey … and Julia … and Rachel … and that one girl—what was her name? Melissa? Who else am I missing, Scott? I know there's more than that."

"I've only been with you!"

"Just tell me the fucking truth!" she cried as she furiously began punching me in the face and chest.

I raised my arms to attempt to block her punches, but it was futile. Her punches landed on my stomach, chest, arms, and face, and even though she was petite, they fucking hurt.

I backpedaled to avoid the barrage of punches, but she continued to advance on me. I was finally pinned against the wall with Claire still swinging at me. I decided to grab her arms and throw her back onto her bed to avert the current situation, but there was one problem with that. I underestimated my strength. I threw her with such force that she bounced off the bed, flew into a bookshelf, and landed on the floor. Books, CD cases, and various knick-knacks toppled off the bookshelf and onto her head and floor.

The room became eerily quiet. We were both shocked. I ran over to help her up onto the bed.

"I am so sorry, Claire!"

"Get the fuck out of my house!" she screamed as she started throwing various items at me.

"Claire! I swear I didn't mean to do that!" I said as I dodged a CD case that was coming directly at my neck.

"If you don't get out of my house this fucking second, I am going to call the cops and tell them you are a drug dealer!"

She knew exactly what to say to get me to leave. I turned and walked out of her room.

That was the last time I saw Claire.

Friday, April 11ᵗʰ

I was sitting in my truck parked in a dimly lit apartment complex in Lakewood, a few blocks south of Colfax. There was a constant buzzing noise from one of the streetlights that flickered on and off.

I was nervously tapping my fingers on the steering wheel to "Nothing Else Matters" by Metallica, attempting to keep a steady rhythm. Mark was sitting next to me and staring blankly out the passenger window. He had not said a word for at least twenty minutes.

"You still up for this?" I asked.
"Yeah."

His response gave me little faith that he would actually go through with the plan when the time was ready.

I was patiently waiting in this lot because Brad called me a few hours before to inform me that Rex was purchasing two 8-balls of crystal from an acquaintance.

"Jack the motherfucker. He did it to you. Now it's your turn," Brad said.
"Fuck, I don't know about this," I responded.
"Don't be a bitch. This guy stole over $1,000 from you, and you don't want fucking payback? I know for a fact he's picking up at least two 8-balls. Go get what's yours!"
"I do want payback, but what if something goes wrong?"
"How about this? I'm going to give you the details. If you want to be a man and get your shit back, use them. If you want to be a little bitch, just pretend like you're writing it down."
"Let me go grab a pen."
"That's what I like to hear."

After I hung up the phone, I conceived a plan to ambush Rex when he walked back to his car after completing the deal. Mark and

I would surround him holding Louisville Sluggers. I'd demand all his crystal and vanish before he knew what happened. I figured the entire process should take less than a minute. No one gets hurt.

On paper, it seemed foolproof. In reality, it scared the shit out of me.

I wanted my revenge, but I had never threatened anyone before. In fact, the closest thing to a fight I had been in was a playground brawl in the fifth grade.

I considered all the different possibilities that could go wrong:

1. He could have a gun or knife.
2. He could have a group of tweakers with him.
3. A police car could be doing a random check of the parking lot.
4. He was secretly a ninja and could knock us out cold.

We had been waiting for over an hour, and I was starting to wonder if Rex was even there. It seemed too easy: threaten him, take the crystal, and run away with a pocket full of drugs and no repercussions. I began wondering why Brad had a vested interest in me retrieving my lost property and thought that it might be a setup. I considered abandoning the plan when a figure emerged from between two buildings.

"Fuck, I think that's him," I whispered as I hit Mark in the shoulder.
"Are you sure?"
"I don't know."
"Well, you better fucking figure it out right now!"

Both of us leaned into the windshield to get a better view. Deep down I really did not want this to be him, but I already knew it was.

"Yeah, that's him. Let's go."

I pulled down the black ski mask and adjusted the eyeholes so they were in the correct viewing position.

"You ready?" I asked Mark.

He nodded.

I reached down to grab the Louisville Slugger and opened the door. I stepped out onto the pavement and then walked to the front of my truck to wait for Mark. As I waited, my breathing became irregular, and I started to hyperventilate. I was getting lightheaded and almost fainted, but I leaned against the truck to prevent my fall.

I sat on the front bumper and leaned against the grill, taking deep breaths in an attempt to stabilize my breathing pattern. The ski mask was restricting my air flow, so I pulled it up over my lips and started gasping for air.

"What the fuck are you doing? Get your fucking shit together!"

I jumped up and pulled down the ski mask, took a practice batting swing, and started running toward the figure in the parking lot.

....

I stopped a few blocks from Mark's house, put the truck in park, and then switched off the headlights. The drive from Lakewood to Littleton was a blur; everything from the moment I ran into the parking lot was a blur.

I glanced down at my right hand and noticed a cut. I had no clue how it happened. I wiped it on my pants in an attempt to remove the blood.

Bits and pieces were starting to come back to me. I remembered running through the parking lot zigzagging between cars. I remembered demanding Rex to get down on the "fucking pavement." I remembered reaching into his pants pocket and pulling out the baggies of meth. And finally I remembered that neither of us had to swing a bat. He followed our commands and seemed as scared as we did. I was thankful no one got hurt.

I felt this was as low as I could get, and the guilt and remorse started to consume me. I wanted the night to be over, so I reached into my pockets and placed the baggies on the seat dividing us.

"Here, one of these is yours. Take whatever one you want," I said. "Thanks. I'll talk to you later."

Mark picked up a baggie then put it into his pocket and got out of my truck. I watched as he walked down the sidewalk and vanished around the corner.

That was the last time I saw Mark.

Saturday, April 12th

After dropping Mark off, I drove home and locked myself in my room with the 8-ball, a GE 40-watt light bulb, and an orange Bic lighter. I sat on the edge of my bed with my crystal supplies next to me and glanced up at the alarm clock. It was 1:41 a.m.

I opened up the baggie and dumped a few rocks into the bulb. I stared down at the bulb between my legs and quickly determined the amount would not suffice. I began dumping more and more crystal into the tiny opening until there was a massive mound resting at the bottom of the glass. I tilted the bulb back and forth to evenly distribute the crystal.

I ignited the flame and inhaled as much smoke as my lungs could consume without coughing. I closed my mouth and focused on not exhaling. My eyes began watering as pressure built up within my chest; it felt like I was holding my breath underwater. As I was about to pass out, I finally exhaled.

I placed the bulb back onto my lap and rested until I resumed a normal breathing pattern. I then picked up the smoking tools and prepared myself for another hit, repeating this process over and over again, all night long. One hit turned into twenty, and minutes turned into hours.

I took the final hit and dropped the bulb onto the floor. It was 6:47 a.m.

I placed my right index finger onto my left wrist to gauge my pulse. I felt nothing. My breathing started to fade, and my eyelids felt heavy. I was tired and just wanted to rest.

I was about to lie down on my bed when the phone began ringing.

I attempted to extend my arm for the cordless receiver, but it felt like I was floating outside my body, watching myself struggle to reach the phone that was only a few feet away. After countless rings, I grasped the phone, placed it against my ear, and pressed the on button.

"Hello?" I said in a weakened voice, unsure if I imagined the ringing sound.
"Scott! Listen to me!"
"Who is this?"
"It's Jake! How fucking high are you?" he yelled into the phone.
"I don't know."
"Well, you better get your shit together and listen to me right fucking now!"
"What?"
"Mark just called and told me that John found his crystal stash and said he got it from you!"
"What?"
"John's on his way to your house right fucking now!"

He said a trigger word, and I sprang up off the mattress.

"John is on his way here?" I asked, unsure if I heard him correctly.
"Mark just called me crying and said he was sorry and that he had no choice."
"What the fuck am I supposed to do?"
"Well, if I were you I'd hang up the phone right fucking now and grab anything and everything that contains meth, has meth residue, or reminds you of meth and then get the fuck out of there!
"Fuck, fuck, fuck!"
"I am hanging up. I suggest you do the same. You probably only have a couple minutes until he gets there. Good luck!"
"Later!" I said as I dropped the phone onto the floor.

I frantically searched for my backpack while trying to remember every location I had hidden a baggie, a piece of tin foil, a light bulb, or any other do-it-yourself crystal device. I wasn't sure if I should leave with the meth I had or spend a few minutes searching for paraphernalia. The last thing I wanted was to be inside the house when he arrived.

"That fucking cocksucker!" I screamed.

Time was against me. I grabbed the remaining 8-ball of crystal off my nightstand and securely placed it into the front pocket of my jeans. I grabbed my backpack, threw it over my shoulder and ran out my room and up the stairs, jumping them four at a time.

When I reached the top of the stairs, I stopped and looked over at my mom who was standing in front of the oven cooking Saturday morning breakfast.

"Are you going somewhere? I was about to make breakfast," she said with a spatula in hand.

I didn't have the courage to respond. I knew in a few minutes John could be at the front door, and she would have to explain why her son had crystal methamphetamine in her house.

I dropped my head and cowardly ran out without uttering a word.

....

I had been to only two funerals in my life. The first one I attended was for my grandpa when I was ten. He had taken a short afternoon walk, and upon his return, decided to take a quick nap before dinner. He lay down and never woke up. He died of a heart attack in his sleep.

Less than a year after my grandpa passed, my uncle proposed to his girlfriend. She simply said no and ended the relationship. He proceeded to drive to a local gun store where he purchased a handgun and bullets. He then drove back to her house, removed the gun from his jacket, and shot her once in the chest without any warning. He then put the gun against his temple and pulled the trigger. Neighbors called 911, and she was rushed to a local hospital in critical condition. She survived, but he was dead on arrival of a self-inflicted gunshot.

As I grew older, I surmised that I suffered from the same depression gene that ultimately ended my uncle's life. I secretly had my own battles with suicide and on numerous occasions had a knife resting on my wrist or a bottle of sleeping pills on the nightstand. My crystal meth addiction seemed to intensify the depression, and the more crystal I did, the closer I got to my own wrecking point.

....

After I left my house, I drove for an hour throughout neighborhoods in south Denver. I was paranoid that I didn't escape in time and the police were trailing me, waiting for the ideal location and time to unleash a surprise attack.

I played out the scenario in my head over and over again. I would pull up to a stop sign, and the cops would surround me in undercover vehicles, leaving me with no possibilities of escape. They would jump out of their vehicles and draw their weapons. I'd calmly say a little prayer, open my door, and charge the closest officer while wielding a box cutter in hopes I would get shot with a single bullet to the head. Suicide by cop, quick and easy.

After a few hours of driving, I finally came to the realization that I was not being followed. I wasn't going to get the easy way out, and that disappointed me.

I continued driving throughout Denver until the red low-fuel light appeared on my dashboard. I knew I was running on fumes, so I turned into a gas station. I parked, walked into the store, and removed the final remnants of cash I had in my wallet—a five-dollar bill. I was now officially flat broke. My savings and checking were at zero, and all my drug money was gone. I handed it to the cashier, smiled, and walked back to my truck to begin the fueling process.

I leaned against my truck while holding the nozzle and looked upward. The sun vanished behind an endless grouping of gray clouds that were producing a steady drizzle. I decided that it would be fitting to end the journey where it all began ten months ago.

I arrived at Miller's Crossing as the sun was setting behind the Rocky Mountains. I pulled into the dirt parking lot facing west so I could gaze upon the beautiful Colorado sunset. I watched the sun set behind the foothills and the sky turn from gray to blue to yellow to orange—until everything faded to black.

It felt like I had not stopped and watched a sunset since I was a little kid. I became sad that I didn't take more time out of my life to stop and fully appreciate tiny moments like that. I closed my eyes and leaned my forehead against the steering wheel, listening as the drizzle gradually turned into a downpour.

I took that as a sign and concluded it was time to commence my endgame.

I unzipped my backpack and removed a box cutter, and placed it on my right thigh. I pushed up on the lever of the orange box cutter and extended the razor blade to the maximum length, about an inch over the safety guard. The metal blade still had meth residue on the edges.

I looked down and watched as the cutter fell off my thigh onto the seat. My legs were shaking so violently that my knees were almost hitting each other. I placed my hands on top of my thighs in an attempt to subdue the tremors, but that only resulted in my entire body shaking. I decided that was a battle I could not win, so I gave up trying.

I raised my left arm toward my face and exhaled onto my inner wrist. That was relaxing and somewhat calmed my nerves. I closed my eyes and repeated the process while I blindly picked up the box cutter with my right hand. I gradually placed the blade against my wrist, sliding it back and forth.

I tilted the box cutter vertically and felt the sharp blade against my skin, veins, arteries, and tendons. I slowly applied downward pressure to the blade and could almost feel it open up my skin when I suddenly stopped.

I began crying. All I wanted to do was slice open my wrist, but I could not bring myself to do it. I attempted three more times to no avail.

"You fucking pussy! Just fucking do it!"

I took a moment to regroup. I exhaled then swiftly lifted the cutter and held the blade to my jugular as if to trick myself into making the incision along my throat. I knew if I did it in one quick motion, like ripping off a Band-Aid, everything would be over in a moment before I had a chance to reconsider.

"I'm so fucking sorry, Mom, Dad, Jim, everyone! I love you guys! I'm sorry!" I was crying so intensely that the words were barely recognizable.

I tilted my head as far back as possible searching for the ideal location. I caressed the blade against my neck and felt the cold metal against my skin every time I swallowed.

One simple movement and I would be dead. My life would abruptly be over, and at that point, I was unsure if my life mattered or if anyone would care. I leaned my head against the driver's side window with the blade securely against my neck and conceded that those would be my final few breaths.

I opened my eyes to get one last view of the world and noticed that from the combination of the rain, the outside temperature, and my heavy breathing, the inside of my windows had fogged up. I lifted my left hand up and extended my index finger, placing it directly in the middle of the window. I wrote one simple, final goodbye message in the fog.

I'm sorry

I closed my eyes and exhaled.

Spring 1998

Wednesday, April 22nd

I was reading *The Denver Post*, and a story caught my eye.

A suspect in a double shooting that left one man dead and another wounded was arrested late Tuesday night. The shooting occurred about 1 a.m. Tuesday morning near the entrance of the Dakota apartments in the 9000 block of West Cross Drive, just north of the Southwest Plaza mall.

I continued reading, and they named Brad as the suspect. At first, I could not believe it. I couldn't imagine him shooting two people over a meth deal gone wrong.

I started making calls to people who I thought might have information of what transpired. The details were vague, and it seemed no one had an accurate story. The following is what I pieced together:

Brad purchased a large amount of crystal from two guys, but it turned out the crystal was bunk. Brad was furious, so he developed a plan to get his revenge. He waited a few days then had a friend set up a meeting to purchase crystal from the two guys. The meeting was in an apartment parking lot located a few blocks from Brad's parents' house.

The guys were waiting in their car when Brad ambushed them. He fired five rounds, shooting both of them multiple times. One of the guys crawled to a nearby apartment where he banged on a front door, and the resident called 911. The guy who summoned help died on the scene, and the other guy was in serious, but stable condition.

The guy who survived identified Brad as the shooter, and he was arrested a few hours later at his parents' house on first-degree murder and attempted-murder charges. If he is convicted on murder charges, he would face either life without parole or the death penalty. Brad is only twenty-one years old, a few months older than me.

If this was true, Brad is never going to be released from jail; he is going to die in prison, be it the death penalty or old age or a prison stabbing. He is never going to be a free man again.

I was numb; this could easily have been me if I continued on my trajectory. It scared the shit out of me just thinking about it. I read the story a few more times then placed the paper on the kitchen table and went on a walk.

....

I was about ten seconds from slicing my throat last April when I looked into the rearview mirror and noticed something I had never seen at Miller's: headlights driving in my direction. I was stunned. In the two years I had been going there, that was the first time I had seen a car driving down the deserted road. I got scared and drove away.

I continued driving until I spotted a dumpster behind a Safeway. I parked next to it and exited my truck with my backpack in hand. I opened the lid and placed the backpack inside the green metal container. I held the lid open with one hand and firmly grasped the strap with the other. My remaining crystal was in the backpack, and I knew if I dropped it, I would have to climb into the dumpster and crawl around in the trash to retrieve it.

I released the strap, and walked away without turning back. I felt liberated, and I smiled, realizing that everything might be okay.

It has been 375 days since that night. That was the last time I used crystal methamphetamine.

I just stopped using. I wish I had a better explanation, but I don't. I stopped as fast as I started. I haven't had the slightest craving to relapse and consider myself extremely fortunate because I didn't need rehab or a drug counselor or a twelve-step program. I just needed to reach my own wrecking point—a shiny orange box cutter against my jugular.

I figured on a long enough timeline there would only be two possible outcomes: prison or death. If I continued using, I would overdose, get murdered, murder someone else, or kill myself. The thought of one of those possible outcomes scared me straight.

Call it destiny, call it fate, call it whatever the fuck you want. I somehow escaped the situation almost unscathed. I'm sure I did irreversible damage to my body, health, and mind, but I am still breathing and not behind prison bars. I could have easily ended up like Brad or the guy he murdered.

I know I have to keep my head up and keep fighting, and as long as I wake up to sunlight on my face, the smell of fresh air, and can see the clear blue sky, I will consider myself lucky. That is all I can hope for because when everything is said and done, we all die and end up in the same place. I guess all that matters is what you do during your short time here.

Made in the USA
Monee, IL
02 July 2022

98950763R00152